1992

I N D I A N

REVOLTS IN NORTHERN NEW SPAIN

A Synthesis of Resistance (1680-1786)

ROBERTO MARIO SALMON
University of Texas, Pan American

UNIVERSITY
PRESS OF
AMERICA

Lanham • New York • London

Copyright © 1991 by

University Press of America®, Inc.

4720 Boston Way
Lanham, Maryland 20706

3 Henrietta Street
London WC2E 8LU England

Library of Congress Cataloging-in-Publication Data

Salmón, Roberto Mario, 1941-
Indian revolts in northern New Spain : a synthesis
of resistance,1680-1786 / Roberto Mario Salmón.
p.   cm.
Includes bibliographical references and index.
1. Indians of Mexico—Mexico, North—Wars.
2. Indians of Mexico—Mexico, North—Government relations.
3. Indians of Mexico—Mexico, North—History.
4. Mexico—History—Spanish colony, 1540-1810.
I. Title.
F1219.1.M64S34   1990   972'.1—dc20   90–44576 CIP

ISBN 0–8191–7982–5 (alk. paper)
ISBN 0–8191–7983–3 (pbk. : alk. paper)

For Shannon
You were with us through it all

CONTENTS

LIST OF ILLUSTRATIONS

Figures

Map

PREFACE

Much of Spain's colonial history in the Americas can be told in terms of the relations between Spaniards, mixed-blood frontiersmen, and Indians. The New World Indians figured as significantly in determining the nature and direction of Spanish advance and settlement as did political and geographical factors. Spaniards were ever desirous to learn more about these Indian peoples, especially if they had cultures and economies worth exploiting. But not all Indians submitted peacefully to strange men who spoke of God or king and insisted on a new way of life. Many Indian leaders only reluctantly gave up positions of tribal control and remained prepared to foment sedition and rebellion against Spanish or mestizo intruders. This resistance occurred most often on the fringes of the Spanish American frontier.

I will, then, survey and evaluate Indian revolts in northern New Spain during the years 1680-1786 in terms of specific Indian revolts, Spanish Indian policy over time, and relations between Spaniards, mestizo frontiersmen, and Indians. In this study, northern New Spain refers to what is now the Mexican North and the southwestern United States. This northern frontier came to encompass the provinces of Nueva Vizcaya, New Mexico, Sonora, Coahuila, Texas, Sinaloa, Sonora, and the two Californias. This territory eventually became a separate, distinct administrative unit of colonial Spanish America.

The northern frontier of New Spain had long seen Indian rebellions. Before the middle of the eighteenth century, the newly named interior provinces--the Provincias Internas del Norte--witnessed no fewer than twelve major uprisings. Each devastating upheaval cost the Spanish Crown thousands of pesos and seriously drained frontier manpower. The overextended Hapsburgs could ill afford such expenditures or loss of men, but after the Bourbons came to power in the eighteenth century, Spain rarely retreated in the face of Indian hostilities. She may have lost the battles, but she won the so-called war. This is well-illustrated by the outcome of Indian uprisings and guerrilla resistance along the northern frontiers of New Spain.

Indian rebellions on the northern borderlands were responses from tribal groups to increased pressure from missionaries, Spanish frontiersmen, Indian colonists, merchants, miners, free and slave blacks and mulattoes, and the complexity of Spanish colonial society itself. As northern tribes felt the limits placed on them by various frontier institutions become increasingly inflexible and more encompassing, they resorted to revolts and guerrilla warfare, attempting to reestablish the balance with frontier society that they believed was slipping away. The alliances that many tribesmen insisted on when they first agreed to allow missionaries, stock herding or mining interest into their country seemed to be violated by the ever-intruding frontier peoples. At every turn, the northern tribes found themselves threatened with loss of land, political autonomy, and their cultural identity.

ix

Missions and presidios receive some discussion here, but my purpose is not to write mission-presidio history as such, and I dwell on these institutions only as they affect the northern tribes. I attempt no analysis of the theological questions concerning the genuineness of the conversion of Indians to the Roman Catholic faith, nor do I intend to present a concise Indian history of the region. I examine instead those aspects of northern New Spain that caused both Spain and Indians to lose the encounter. For those wishing a more concise introduction to Spanish/Indian relations in northern New Spain, I recommend the works of Philip Wayne Powell on the Chichimeca or María del Carmen Velásquez on Spanish/Indian relations on the far northern frontier.

By way of acknowledgments, I wish to thank my wife, Mary Salmón for the time and effort in criticizing the manuscript version of this study. I am indebted to her for corrections and help in improving style and content. I would also like to thank Eva Gomez and Joel A. Garza for their help in laying out the final copy of this work. Finally, this manuscript began as a dissertation which has incorporated additional research and has shared findings through published research. A part of Chapter 4 appeared as "Tarahumara Resistance to Mission Congregation in Northern New Spain, 1580-1710," in Ethnohistory (Fall 1977): 379-93. Chapter 5 is an extended research effort of "Frontier Warfare in the Hispanic Southwest, Tarahumara Resistance, 1649-1780," appearing in Mid-America, An Historical Review 58 (October 1976): 175-85. Reprinted by permission. Part of Chapter 5 appears as "A Marginal Man: Luis of Saric and the Pima Revolt of 1751," in The Americas, A Quarterly Review of Inter-American Cultural History (July 1988): 61-77. Reprinted by permission. Also, parts of Chapter 9 will appear in Military History of the Southwest.

Roberto Mario Salmón
University of Texas, Pan American
Edinburg, Texas
Fall 1990

CHAPTER I

SETTLEMENT OF
NORTHERN NEW SPAIN

Spanish expansion in North America was decidedly dynamic until abruptly halted in the Mexican North and the American Southwest. Indian resistance by nomadic tribes and first submission then revolts by sedentary Indian communities delayed the extension of Spanish colonial society. Communities the Spaniards for almost two centuries considered politically and culturally inferior to the Aztecs of central Mexico took the offensive, baffled defending Spanish mixed-blood soldiery, broke the chain of ineffective presidios established to control them, and terrorized the harried colonizers. Indian warriors exacted high tolls in commerce, livestock, and lives. Yet the frontier stereotypes differ much from our usual image of heroes and villains, and despite their virtues or faults, both frontiersman and Indian believed they fought to preserve a way of life. The irony of the struggle is the degree to which it shaped a common culture.

Spaniards and their Mexican allies brought a variety of influences to northern New Spain. They planted new crops, in the process denuding some of the forested mountain slopes, and introduced livestock, adding grazing areas to the land used by the Indians. The association of livestock raising with nobility predisposed many civilian settlers to careers in ranching, and the discovery of great silver mines in Hidalgo, Zacatecas, and Guanajuato increased the demand for hides, tallow, meat, and draft animals--further incentive for Spanish expansion northward.[1] Much energy and attention soon focused on this advance, and cattle, sheep, and goats often accompanied Spanish settlements.

The north, with its vast expanses of unoccupied grass and brushland, especially suited cattle-raising. By the eighteenth century, animal population increased impressively in the frontier provinces of Nueva Vizcaya, Nuevo Mexico, Sinaloa, Sonora, Coahuila, Texas, Nuevo León, and Nuevo Santander (present American states of Texas, New Mexico, and Arizona, and Mexican states of Coahuila, Chihuahua, Durango, Sonora, and Sinaloa).[2] Although the two Californias and Tamaulipas also came under the designation Northern New Spain, their association with the more interior provinces remained nominal. In the late eighteenth century, the first five were named Provincias Internas del Norte, and over them was set in motion the dynamics of Indian revolts and resistance.

Spaniards, Indians, and Blacks who migrated to the Provincias Internas represented almost every type found in New Spain, and seeking opportunity, they quite naturally sought the farthest corners of the northern frontier. The rank and file were not representative Caucasians (europeos, españoles, or criollos), but came from all ethnic levels and mixtures of society, and this diversity of their settlement and possibility for large-scale preemptive acquisition of land helped promote development of a small class of settler-stockman types of frontier origin.[3] The settlement process, usually quite egalitarian, was strongly characterized by the private initiative of miners or hacendados (Spanish landowners), the rise of mestizo military leaders from the presidio ranks, and the kind of group action found in most frontier communities.[4] The civilian settlers' (or pobladores) proximity to the Indian war, and their opinion of Spanish officials charged with enforcing the king's humanitarian Indian policy catalyzed the politics of wilderness diplomacy.

Spanish officials, such as the Marqués del Castillo, normally served the Christian-Humanist goals of Spanish colonization in the New World, but in various efforts to populate Northern New Spain, they allowed many compromises in Indian welfare, especially in areas not densely populated by Indians. The crown's long tradition of Indian legislation included the Laws of Burgos in 1513, the New Laws in 1542, and the Recopilación de leyes de los reynos de las Indias (the general laws of the Indies) in 1681. As the frontier expanded northward, these laws appeared petty and dated, yet the Recopilación was relied on repeatedly;[5] the Audiencia de Guadalajara, under Castillo's presidency, used it as a firm basis of policy in dealing with the Seri, Pima, Yaqui, and Apache enemies.

Spanish officials, as close to the Indian wars as the pobladores, included José de Gálvez, dispatched to New Spain in 1765 as visitor general with viceregal powers; the Marqués de Rubí, a field marshal with the military mission carrying instructions to inspect the presidios of the north; Captain Nicolás de Lafora, who kept a diary of the Rubí inspection; the Irishman, Lieutenant Colonel Hugo O'Conor, commandant inspector and experienced frontier officer in Spain's royal army, who from headquarters in Nueva Vizcaya launched two general campaigns against the Apache nation; the Caballero Teodoro de Croix, O'Conor's successor; Bernardo de Gálvez; and Jacobo Ugarte y Loyola.

In contrast to these officials were the missionaries: Father Juan Agustín Morfí, who left an excellent account of his travels; Eusebio Francisco Kino, Junípero Serra and Francisco Garcés, who worked for Christian conversion of the Indians on the outreaches of the northern frontier. Of prime importance, also arrived front-line persuaders of peace: Juan Bautista de Anza, Domingo Díaz, Nicolás Gil, Francisco Martínez, and Rafael Martínez Pacheco. These officers saw the war for what it was--a sporadic, temporary, and limited peacemaking between Spaniard, Indian, and mixed-blood frontiersmen.

Spanish colonists in the northern provinces clearly proved their self-sufficiency, but landed estates and productive mines were difficult to maintain without Indian cooperation. Because of this, pobladores, of whatever blood, hungered for peace, and from past experience, expected stability to follow after each military victory over the Indians. This seems to be their great misunderstanding in the northern frontier. Whenever northern tribes found it advantageous to sue for peace, whether because of military weakness or disease, they willingly submitted to the various missionary endeavors around them or settlement near presidios or civilian communities to heal their wounds and observe Spanish action. The Spaniards and their Mexican allies, confident of a long awaited

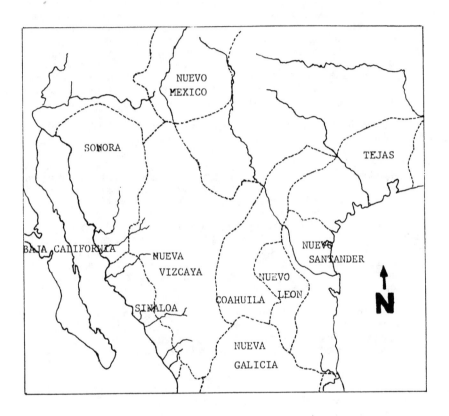

Northern New Spain, 1700

peace, almost invariably advanced northward, immediately causing an economic boom and a decline in military preparedness which invited rebellion. Indian warriors accepted such invitations without delay.

The amount and pervasiveness of conflict within this frontier society deeply impressed Spanish officials. Invading tribesmen, emerging from the safety of mountain retreats, terrorized <u>villas</u> (chartered towns), mining camps, haciendas, small ranches, farms, and shepherds and <u>vaqueros</u>, or cowboys, tending their animals.[6] Indian warriors sought cattle as a source of food and clothing, and horses. First introduced into the Americas by Spaniards, the horse revolutionized Indian warfare and held great cultural value, increasing the status and influence of the warrior owning one or many. Firearms, obtainable after the Pueblo Revolt of 1680, also because valued acquisitions but prior to the mid 1700s, no tribe had sufficient supply to make good use of them, and in general, possession of such a weapon remained simply a status symbol.[7]

Drawn by the protection the presidio offered, and tormented by murder, property loss, and constant insecurity, many a frontier family settled at or near its defenses. Yet many remained in isolated settlements or at abandoned presidio sites in frontier communities away from immediate protection.[8] Indian warriors appreciated the future advantage represented by a live, isolated poblador who would raise more stock for next year's raid. But the "northerners," whose mixed-blood legacy was hardly passive, frequently banded together to scour Indian territory. Such counter-expeditions were not punitive but had the same objectives as the raids from which they suffered.[9] The frontiersmen sought stock, plunder, and captives destined for sale as slaves in civilian households. Once contact was made, methods of combat rivaled in barbarity those employed by the victims. Such attacks hurt guilty and innocent alike, and usually the reprisal in turn set off a counter-reprisal. Frontiersmen responded to the Indian menace with both passive defense and savage offense.

The strands of European, Mexican, and Indian life became tightly interwoven in a fabric of unique and partly cynical relationships. Indian warriors robbed, terrorized butchered Spanish pobladores. On the same scale, the colonists visited the same cruelties upon Indians. Some supplied arms and ammunition to the Indians who used them to slaughter other frontier peoples. This pattern, well-fixed by the 1750s and not easily broken by the Bourbons created for the Spanish sovereignty, represented by men such as Juan Francisco de la Puerta, one of the most stubborn obstacles to the Indian Wars. Like others before him, Governor Puerta realized that this was not simply a war of Spaniards versus Indians.[10]

The troublesome dilemma on the frontier involved a <u>guerra de fuego y a sangre</u> (war by fire and blood) versus kingly humanitarian treatment of the Indians. An outspoken segment of the frontier population viewed the Indians as faithless and uncivilized, unworthy of sympathy or understanding.[11] But many officers and men, especially those born and raised in the northern provinces, though seeing the Apaches, Tarahumaras, or Pimas as inferior, still considered them human beings who suffered great wrongs. Frontiersmen in the more outlying districts demanded a guerra de fuego y a sangre against Indian hostilities, even to the point of perpetual enslavement. Decisive action, however, enraged a keenly sensitive Spanish sovereignty. And career soldiers, such as Juan Bautista de Anza, apparently struggling with their consciences and buffeted by extremes of opinion, had to battle an enemy with whom, in many cases, they sympathized in military forays provoked by their own people.[12]

Another problem confronted by presidios as well as frontier people in general lay in the great degree of policy control by enlightened vested interest. To an extent, the northerners themselves, dependent on the frontier's economic development, were such a vested interest. The Spanish frontiersman of northern New Spain looked to the presidios as a legitimate form of labor or profit. Soldiering was far better than starving from lack of frontier work, and despite the usually ensuing indebtedness, credit remained good at the presidio store, and the soldier's family received protection from the garrison. By the 1760s, all twenty-three garrisons, except for the privately financed presidio of El Paseje, had significant Indian and mestizo settlements.[13] But profit-making pressures originated mostly from Spanish or mestizo traders, contractors, freighters, and private financiers whose gains derived from royal expenditures for feeding and fighting the Indians. The location of presidios and size of their garrison often owed as much to commercial aspirations disguised under exaggerations of Indian danger as to legitimate Bourbon reforms. In Nueva Vizcaya, four mercantile houses at Chihuahua monopolized the presidial supply business by 1783. One provincial governor accumulated more than eight thousand pesos in eight years from provisioning the troops, and had made a profit of as much as one thousand per cent on some items.[14] Shaping military policies and actions to fit needs assessed by military rather than commercial interests remained unsolved problems for front-line field commanders.

Not all Indians inhabiting the northern provinces in the seventeenth and eighteenth century opposed the frontier armed forces. In 1760, according to Bishop Pedro Tamarón y Romeral, the total frontier population numbered 233,600, with fewer than half of these Indian. Nueva Vizcaya was home for 47,150 Indians; Sonora had 54,000; New Mexico 9,400; Coahuila 1,400; and Texas 1,500--a total Indian population of 113,500.[15] Some of them, such as the Mayos and Opatas, accommodated the Spanish presence. Others, such as the Conchos, Tobosos, Tarahumaras, and coastal Seris of Sonora, fought Spanish in the past and continued to do so. Still others, such as the Salineros, Tamaulipas, Tortugas, and Venados, terrorized by more powerful tribes and decimated by contagious diseases introduced by Spain and her allies, never gathered the strength to fight. In 1760, only a handful of tribes retained the power and will to contest the northward advancement. On the plains of Texas were the Comanches and the so-called Nations of the North (Taovayas, Wichitas, Kichais, Iscanis, Tawakonis, and others). New Mexico had Comanches, Utes, Navajos, and the several Apache nations classified according to locale and customs. The Conchos, Tobosos, Tarahumaras, Mescalero Apaches, and renegade Indian bands roamed Nueva Vizcaya. In Coahuila were the Lipán Apaches, and in Sonora, the Seris, Upper Pimas, Gileño Apaches, and Yumas. These Indian hostiles engaged the Spanish side in this war throughout the remaining decades of the century.

Culturally, Indian peoples differed markedly from one another in language, political and social organization, and religion. The highly mobile bands of

Shoshone-speaking Indians, known as the Comanches, ranged over vast distances in search of game--usually small game which satisfied their primary needs of food, shelter, clothing, and utensils. In contrast, Apache desert and plateau dwellers, such as the Coyoteros of the Sierra Madre Occidental, lived in compact bands, traveled largely on foot, and subsisted, part of the time, on irrigated or dry farm agriculture. Mountain bands, such as the Tontos, Chiricahuas, Mimbreños, and Mogolloñes, influenced by both plains and plateau groups, also developed special characteristics of their own. Most Indian societies, however, were generally associated with a low material culture. They had little access to the production of surplus, little need for specialists or elites, and were far removed from large population centers.

For most Indian communities, land ownership was communal. Usage rights were family based and established through headrights or, rancheria (loosely organized communities) claims. Each ranchería extended family was self-sufficient with all members actively involved in maintaining economic subsistence. It basically was collective agricultural existence, living from harvest to harvest and resorting to hunting and gathering in order to keep away from a food crisis. Opatas, Pimas, Yaquis, and Tarahumaras were a ranchería people. They lived off the staple crops of maize, beans, and squash, the dispersed pattern of settlement clearly most convenient to this system of food production. Indians of the north were scattered widely over the land, limited in their spacing only by the occurrence of water sources.

In pre-Hispanic times, Indian communities had flexible territorial limits. Communities restricted membership to people born and raised within their local boundaries, and rules of community marriage further limited the immigration of new members. Membership in the community was also demonstrated by participation in religious rituals conducted by shamans or medicine men. In the Indian world, each community maintained the proper relations with its spirits and ancestors. Totemic rituals which served this function could not be performed by the individual. Each year lands were ritually purified, community spirits were feasted and offerings were made to the souls of the dead. The religious leaders, usually a leader of great stature or a respected medicine man, were considered personifications of the spiritual relationship of the Indians to their land.

Many Indian people believed that everything, including man-made objects, had a soul. The concept of soul, especially the soul lost as the result of witchcraft or sorcery, was the center of several northern religions. "Guardian spirits" that resided in the earth, rivers and sky exerted control over trade, travel, war, disease and other aspects of human life. The wind, for example, was a good spirit; the rainbow was sent by evil underground sorcerers; a shooting star was a sorcerer flying to seize souls. These spirits, both guardian and evil, possessed supernatural powers. The belief was held that the guardian spirit could wander and become lost or that someone could even steal it. This "loss of soul" could then lead to depression, sickness, or death. Indian people would call in a shaman or medicine man for such a person, and the hechicero (wizard or witch to the mission fathers) would perform a ceremony to retrieve the guardian spirit and bring the patient back into harmony with himself/herself. Many a skilled hechiceros shared with the bravest of warriors the highest of regard in their communities.

Thus, a shaman could bring spiritual calm and confidence to a band or tribe by helping them to workout any misfortunes that had befallen them. The power of the hechicero's presence led disoriented persons or bands to acknowledge bad or evil actions. As helping spirits, shamans served a leaders to many a northern Indian people. The basic power of their spontaneity and improvisations moved many Indian people to rise in rebellion.

Spanish officials were greatly disturbed by Indian belief in their hechiceros, the term itself being coined by the Society of Jesus. Jesuit fathers had no doubts about the abilities of wizards or about the ability of hechiceros to transform themselves into animals, or to become invisible as they practiced their craft.[16]

Essentially, after 1680 and suppression of the Pueblo Revolt, Indian religions were both a compartmentalization and a blending of Spanish Christianity with northern Indian polytheism. The first was based on the official Church-fiesta; the second was based on a hechicero-ranchería group setting. The Christian elements were heavily overlaid with Indian cultural elements of dance and ritual technique, and despite adherence to the Catholic ceremonial calendar, the resulting ceremonies were an attempt to blend and reconcile two religious philosophies. Indian fiestas, on the other hand, were clearly Indian. The symbolic entities of their fiestas included the souls of the dead, who were greatly feared and were given rich ceremonial recognition.

Like many other self-sufficient societies, northern Indians valued conformity to the extent that a man or woman was judged largely according to his or her ability to live up to unchanging ideas of appropriate behavior. Idiosyncratic behavior was strongly discouraged, except in a few restricted and well-defined social contexts. Indian people greatly feared dishonor and reproach, hence gossip and public criticism were strong factors making for conformity in Indian life. It is wrong, however, to equate intolerance or non-conformity with a lack of respect for individual dignity. Many tribes or bands strongly objected to individuals or groups overly trying to coerce someone to behave contrary to his or her own wishes. If such coercion came from outside the community, it was an affront to the individual's neighbors as well as to himself.[17]

The feelings that Spaniards, Mexicans, and Indians had about one another were influenced by their awareness of physical and cultural differences between them. Physical differences seem to have impressed the Spaniards and their allies more than they did the Indians. For example, Indian men and women were described as well-proportioned, robust and , on the average, shorter than tribes of other areas in the Americas. They were trained from youth to endure hardship and misfortune with patience and fortitude. In dealings with one another, most were gentle and considerate. This self-control may account for the often repeated missionary comment that Indians were "naturally peace loving." Chroniclers frequently stated that the men were lazy. This appears to have been a false impression that arose because of the division of labor among Indians. The Indians were not readily amenable to the kind of routine labor to which the Spanish were accustomed.[18]

The men generally dressed in deerskin and a bonnet of the same material, sometimes adorned with feathers. In hot weather, they wore a breechcloth of deerskin and a pair of soft skin moccasins. Some tribes tattooed their flesh, pierced their noses and painted their faces, arms and legs with chalk and red earth. Generally, Indians were proud of their hair and spent much time caring for it. The Tarahumara, for example, wore their hair long, cutting it only upon the death of a relative. For the most part both men and women went about barefoot. The women also dressed in skins, but with a short skirt tied at the waist and loose at the knees. They adorned themselves with strings of deer hooves, shells, fish spines and fragrant roots around their necks and arms. Complete nudity, common among some band peoples, was frowned upon by other tribes.

There is no question that in pre-Hispanic times the Indian subsistence pattern was predominantly based on agriculture. The duty of the Indian male was to maintain his own land base and to hunt small game whenever necessary. The planting, care and harvesting of food crops were men's tasks. The women, in this division of labor, prepared the foods, made the necessary kitchen utensils, carried water and firewood, collected seeds and fruit and helped keep the fields clean of weeds. Both men and women remained active into old age, performing their respective obligations. In Tarahumara and Tepehuán culture, each male married within his own community. Tarahumaras did not intermarry with neighboring tribes. The small nuclear family met the ideal requirements of Indian life, and each individual household produced most of the food and utensils which it needed. Consequently, there were no strong economic ties holding many band peoples together.

The importance of hunting for the subsistence economy of northern Mexico has been greatly underrated. Hunting served as the principal measure of a man's courage and demonstrated his ability to use weapons. More important, hunting was an activity that was much enjoyed by Indian men. Working fields required energy and devotion, but such activity among many bands did not appear to have been the source of a appreciable amount of prestige in their relationships to one another. In fact, the lessening cultural importance of hunting well may have been a factor promoting a growing interest in war. An apparent decline in tribal warfare after 1680 may reflect the growth of alliances, which served to suppress local warfare. The conflict that continued against the Spaniards indicated that by that time warfare was basic to the social organization of many northern tribes. This is probably because warfare was the principal means by which men gained personal prestige and established a role for themselves in the social and political life of their communities.

In the Indian world, diet was largely vegetarian. Crops accounted for perhaps three-quarters of all food consumed. The basic foodstuffs of maize, beans and squash, as indicated earlier, suggests that the Indians had long cultivated some of the most ancient and important crops known in Mexico and the Southwest, and that they depended on maize, for example, for the preparation of pinole, atole, tortillas and tamales. Domesticated animals, however, played a minor role in the Indian diet. In pre-Hispanic times, small dogs and turkeys were raised and fattened for eating. Wheat and barley were introduced into the northern region in the late seventeenth century, but these crops never became a significant source of food for

PIMA WOMEN
Drawing by Arthur Schott, 1857 (W.H. Emory, Report on the United States and
Mexican Boundary Survey, vol. 1, Washington, D.C., 1857).

YUMAS
Drawing by Arthur Schott, 1857 (W.H. Emory, <u>Report on the United States and Mexican Boundary Survey,</u>   vol. 1, Washington, D.C., 1857).

the Indian. The Jesuit attempt to establish wheat as a source of flour was successfully resisted, as was the introduction of sugar cane in the far western part of northern New Spain.

An egalitarian political structure characterized most Indian groups, and whatever the precise form of Indian organization, authority usually resided in many leaders rather than few. Decisions affecting a small band were made by a council or similar governing body convening many representatives of the people. Occasionally leaders of great personal stature emerged, but they almost always expressed their influence through loose coalitions. With so many voices of authority, and those sharply limited, decisions came hard or not at all. Major questions of peace or war caused much factionalism, with bands and even families pursuing separate courses. Without a ruling class or a political structure, limited and conditional organization set northern Indian communities apart.

Indians warred or rebelled after contact with Spanish frontier society, but not initially. Many Indians' first reaction to incursions into their territory was one of friendly curiosity, and others sought alliance with Spanish representatives against their own enemies. Generally, a period of early contact, during which missionaries, miners or town builders established themselves, was followed by quick, violent uprisings against the pressure of culture contact. This commonly occurred in frontier areas where many Indians considered themselves victims of land encroachment and political dispersion. The area extending from Sonora east across Chihuahua to western Coahuila--roughly the province of Nueva Vizcaya--witnessed the greatest unrest, with Mescalero and Lipán raiders from Texas, New Mexico, and Coahuila striking deep into the districts around Chihuahua, Durango, Saltillo, and Parras.[19] Most hit-and-run raiding originated in the Bolsón de Mapimí, a great longitudinal depression once an ancient seabed. The Bolsón, immediately below the Big Bend region of Texas, pointed directly into the heart of the populated districts. Along its sides ran a series of mountain ranges which accommodated Indian hideaways, and the basin itself served as a highway south for Mescalero forays. Following trails linked by water seeps and meager pasturage, Indian warriors slipped undetected into the heart of Nueva Vizcaya, and struck in every direction.[20]

The province of Coahuila covered a wide terrain stretching from the Medina River of Texas on the northeast to the arroyo de la Pendencia which divided it from Nuevo León on the southeast, and from the Big Bend region of the Río Grande on the northwest to the Bolsón de Mapimí on the southwest. Coahuila had a population base of some 3,150 frontier settlers, clustered together in four villas, three military garrisons, and sixteen rural communities. Tlaxcalan Indians from central Mexico lived in four incorporated pueblos, while six missions served the Indians native to the province. The major towns of Coahuila were Santiago de Monclova and San Fernando de Austria, and had as defense from Indians raids three presidios: Monclova, San Juan Bautista del Río Grande, and Santa Rosa del Sacramento. Rural Indian and mestizo settlements included the community of San Buenaventura; the haciendas of Castano, Carmen, Cuatro Ciénegas, Sardinas, Las Encinas, El Alamo, and La Cauciera; the estates of Santa Tecla, San Pablo, San Miguel, and Santiago; and the ranches of San Vicente, La Casita, El Chocolate, and San Matias. Nadadores and San Francisco were Tlaxcalan pueblos, and towns comprised of Tlaxcalan and other Indians were located in the Valley de la Candela. The Coahuilan missions included San Miguel de Aguayo, San Bernardo, San Juan Bautista, Nombre de Jesús, San Francisco de Bizarrón, and San José del Carrizo.[21]

Nueva Vizcaya, the most beleaguered province, had a population of 70,050 colonizers, scattered around the silver-bearing districts of San José del Parral, Santa Bárbara, Cuencamé, Cusihuiriáchic, and the villa of San Felipe el Real de Chihuahua. Durango, with a large mixed-blood population, was the provincial capital. Fifty-eight rural settlements and thirty-seven missions serving 47,150 Indians completed Nueva Vizcaya's population makeup. Major settlements included Cuencamé, Durango, Papasquiaro, Saltillo, Santa Bárbara, San Juan, Parral, Parras, Chihuahua. Only four presidios existed before 1722: Concepción del Pasaje de Cuencamé (generally called El Pasaje) in the south, San Felipe y Santiago de Janos in the north, the relocated presidio of La Junta de los Ríos in the northeast, and the recently created compañía volante, or mobile company, headquartered at Guajoquiolla (present-day Ciudad Jímenez, Chihuahua) in the east. Rural communities included Analco, Cerro Gordo, El Pasaje, Indé, Mapimí, Nombre de Díos, San Bartolomé, San Buenaventura, and San Francisco de Conchos; the haciendas of Aguilillas, Anelo, Atotonilco, Boquillas, Carmen de Peñablanc, Carrizal, Ciénega de los Olivos, Corral de Piedras, Dolores, Encinillas, El Alamo, Hormigas, Magistral, Navacoyan, Noria, Patos, Ramada, Ramos, Ruíz, San Juan Bautista de Casta, San Lorenzo, San Mateo, Torreón, and Zarca; and the estancias of Becerras, Habas, Patrón, Río Florido, and Santa Rosalia.

Sonora has a population of 35,000 colonizing allies, scattered throughout the province in four villas, six military garrisons, and fourteen rural settlements. In addition were forty-one mining towns and twenty-one missions serving the 54,000 Indians there. The villas of Arizpe and Horcasitas (moved to the new villa of Pitic in 1780) were the major towns, and Sonora's six presidios included San Carlos de Buenavista in the south, San Miguel de Horcasitas in the west, Santa Gertrudis de Altar in the northwest, Fronteras, Terrenate, and San Ignacio de Tubac in the north. Alamos, Calabazas, Guaymas, Pitic, Suaqui, Tumacóori, and Ures were rural communities. Also outlying were the haciendas of Cedros, Lima, Mescatitlan, and Tesopaco; the estancia of San Rafael de Buenavista; and the ranches of Malpica and Ocura. Mission pueblos with considerable race mixture among Opatas, Pimas, and mestizo settlers became situated at Aconchi, Babiacora, Banamichi, Batuco, Guazaba, Guepaca, Matape, Nacori, Oposura, Oputu, Sinoquipe, Tarapa, Tepachi, and Tepuspe.

The initial categories of race and function ceased to coincide in Sonora. Many Indians in the missions suffered uprooting and socialization. The frontier tended to equalize, miscegenation produced a host of mixed types and, as the new society grew, its social and economic functions took priority over biological origin. The resultant racial mix is reflected in the loose term castas, applied to person of "impure caste" and lower social status.[22] By the time of the Bourbon economic reforms, social categorization fully developed to accommodate castas in the northern provinces, while at the same time the expansion of economic life created intermediate avenues of release from servile status. Still, it must be stressed that most non-Indians, no matter how lowly, considered themselves superior to Indians.[23]

New Mexico, excluding El Paso, had a population of 11,000 settlers, clustered in the northern region and distributed into eight major districts. The province had twenty-one rural settlements, seven communities of <u>genízaros</u> (detribalized Indians), and twenty-four missions serving 9,400 Pueblo Indians. New Mexico's major population centers included Santa Fe, Santa Cruz de La Cánada, Albuquerque, and Taos. According to Bishop Tamarón, shocked by conditions in New Mexico, Santa Fe had no formal presidio in 1760.[24] Instead, the 100 or so officers and men were quartered in the town. The larger rural communities included Abiquíu, Belen, Bernalillo, San Miguel del Bado, Socorro, Tomé, and Truchas. Genízaros settled outside Abiquíu, Pojoaque, San Juan, Santa Clara, Taos, Tomé, with one such community living in the barrio of Santa Fe.

Bishop Tamarón recorded Texas' meager population at nine hundred people, settled at or near the five military garrisons and nine missions.[25] Major Texan towns were the Villa de San Fernando, eventually encircling the presidio of San Antonio de Béjar, and Nuestra Señora de Pilar de los Adaes, the nominal capital of Texas. Defense of the province came from five garrisons; San Antonio, Los Adaes, San Luis de Amarillas (known as San Sabá): San Agustín de Ahumada (commonly called Orcoquisac), and La Bahía de Espíritu Santo (also called Nuestra Señora de Loreto). The missions of El Cañon, Espíritu Santo, Nuestra Señora de la Luz, Nuestra Señora del Rosario, San Lorenzo de la Santa Cruz, San Antonio Valero, San Juan Capistrano, Purísima Concepcíon de Acuña, and San José Aguayo served some fifteen hundred Indians.[26]

Thus, Spanish economic development in the far northern provinces, bent on absorbing the Indian world, led to a power struggle with a people who resisted the loss of independent identities, their land, and their communal patterns of existence. Indians, for the most part, sought to survive both within their own cultural patterns and in the Spanish colonial world surrounding them. They demonstrated great courage and resourcefulness in defending their culture and in devising strategies for survival. This struggle in the northern provinces of New Spain kept the frontier in turmoil. Had it not persisted, the history of the southwestern United States would read quite differently.

CHAPTER 1

FOOTNOTES

[1]The distinctive development in the Mexican North is seen in Francois Chevalier, Land and Society in Colonial Mexico; and P.J. Bakewell, Silver Mining and Society in Colonial Mexico Zacatecas 1546-1700.

[2]Alonso de la Mota Escobar, Descripción geográfica de los reinos de Nueva Galicia, Nueva Vizcaya y Nuevo Leon, ed. by Joaquín Ramírez Cabañas, 186-89.

[3]For Coahuila's make-up see Teodoro de Croix's Padrones de matrículas de familias pobladores, Chihuahua, June 1, 1778, Archivo General de Indias, Audiencia de Guadalajara, Legajo 255). For Nueva Vizcaya, see Padrones de Santa Bárbara y San Bartolome en 1775, AGI, Indiferente General 1526. For Sonora, José Maestro y Cuevas's Padron de 2,728 habitantes, Rosario, February 20, 1778, AGI, Indiferente General 102.

[4]See for example Title 11, Articles 1 and 2 of the Reglamento e instrucción para los presidios que se han de formar en la linea de frontera de la Nueva España, resuelto por el Rey Nuestro Señor en cédula de 10 de Septiembre de 1772 (Madrid, 1772). A printed copy appears in AGI, Guadalajara 522 (hereafter cited as Regalamento de 1772). For text and English translation from the Mexico, 1834 printing see Sidney B. Brinckerhoff and Odie B. Faulk, Lancers for the King: A Study of the Frontier Military System of Northern New Spain, with a Translation of the Royal Regulations of 1772.

[5]Plan of the Marqués del Castillo de Aysa, president of the Audiencia de Guadalajara, January 21, 1743, Archivo General de la Nacion, ramo Provincias Internas, Tomo 87 (hereafter cited as AGN, PI 87).

[6]Bishop Pedro Tamarón y Romeral to Minister of the Indies Julian Arriaga, Durango, December 26, 1761, AGI, Guadalajara 511: Luis Navarro García, Don José de Gálvez y la Comandancia General de las Provincias Internas del Norte de Nueva España, 60-63, 80-81.

[7]Viceroy Antonio María Bucareli to Arriaga, No. 736, Mexico, January 27, 1773 (enclosed with Extracto de Novedades from the governor of Texas, the Barón de Ripperdá), AGI, Guadalajara 513.

[8]Maestro de Campo José Francisco Marín to Viceroy Conde De Galve, Parral, September 30, 1693, in Charles W. Hackett, ed., Historical Documents Relating to New Mexico, Nueva Vizcaya, and Approaches Thereto, to 1773, 3 vols., 2:384-409.

[9]Nicolás de Lafora, Relación del viajes que hizo a los Presidios Internos situados en la frontera de la America Septentrional perteneciente al Rey de España, ed. by Vito Alessio Robles, 61-67, 83-84. 113. For an English translation see Lawrence Kinnaird, ed., The Frontiers of New Spain: Nicolás de Lafora's Description, 1766-1768.

10Governor Juan Franciso de la Puerta y Barrera, Testimonios sobre el estado de los presidios ...de esta provincia de la Nueva Vizcaya, Mexico, July 17, 1751 (copy), AGI, Guadalajara 136; Viceroy Bucareli to Arriaga, No. 881, Mexico, April 26, 1773, AGI, Guadalajara 416.

11Juan Lucas de Lazaga to Minister of the Indies José de Gálvez, Mexico, February 28, 1781 (enclosed with Viceroy Martín de Mayorga to Gálvez, No. 1526, Mexico, February 20, 1782), AGI, Guadalajara 519; Ayuntamiento de San Felipe el Real de Chihuahua, December 21, 1767, AGI, Guadalajara 416.

12Diario de Capitán Juan Bautista de Anza, Mexico, June 26, 1774 (certified copy), AGI, Guadalajara 418. A third-generation frontiersman, Anza saw clearly what such a war of extermination as fuego y a sangre implied for the northern tribes. For documents relating to Anza's Indian policy in New Mexico see Alfredo B. Thomas, ed., Forgotten Frontiers: A Study of the Spanish Indian Policy of Don Juan Bautista de Anza, Governor of New Mexico, 1777-1787.

13Max L. Moorhead, The Presidio: Bastion of the Spanish Borderlands, 201, 222-24.

14Ibid., 207, 215-16; Navarro García, Don José de Gálvez, 403.

15Pedro Tamarón y Romeral, Demostración del vastísmo obispado de las Nueva Vizcaya, 1765. Durango, Sinaloa, Sonora, Arizona, Nuevo Mexico, Chihuahua y porciones de Texas, Coahuila y Zacatecas, ed. by Vito Alessio Robles, 149, 176, 363; Navarro García, Don José de Gálvez, 114-118.

16Edward H. Spicer, Cycles of Conquest: The Impact of Spain, Mexico, and the United States on Indians of the Southwest, 310-24.

17For a comparison of band attitudes see Ralph L. Beals, The Comparative Ethnology of Northern Mexico Before 1750; Carl Sauer, the Distribution of Aboriginal Tribes and Languages in Northwestern Mexico; Frederick W. Hodge, ed., Handbook of the American Indians North of Mexico, 2.

18Spicer, Cycles of Conquest, 310-24.

19See José Ignacio Gallegos, Durango colonial, 1563-1821.

20Vito Alessio Robles, Coahuila y Texas en la época colonial, 2 vols., 2: 559-68.

21Max L. Moorhead, The Apache Frontier: Jacobo Ugarte and Spanish-Indian Relations in Northern New Spain, 1769-1791, 26; Lafora, Relación del viaje, 179, 195-200, 203-206, 245.

22Ibid., 266. 284; Mario Hernández y Sánchez-Barba, "Frontera, Población y Milicia (Estudio estructural de la acción defensiva hispánica en Sonoro durante el siglo XVIII)," Revista de Indias 63 (1956): 9-49; Alfred B. Thomas, "A Description of Sonora in 1722," Arizona Historical Review 5 (1932-33): 302-07.

23Pilar Sanchiz Ochoa, "La Población indígena del noroeste de Mexico en el siglo XVIII: algunas cuestiones en torno a la demografía y aculturacíon," Revista española de Antropología Americana 7 (1972): 105-10.

24Copia del Informe General instruido en cumplimiento de Real Orden de 1784. Sobre las misiones del rio de Nueva España comparando su actual estado con el que tenia las que entregaron los ex-jesuitas el tiempo de su expatriacio, 1793, AGI, Guadalajara 578; Sanford A. Musk, "Economic Problems in Sonora in the Late Eighteenth Century," Pacific Historical Review 8 (September 1939): 341-46.

25Eleanor B. Adams, ed., "Bishop Tamarón's Visitation of New Mexico, 1760," part 2 New Mexico Historical Review 28 (July 1953): 206 (Hereafter cited as NMHR).

26Navarro García, Don José de Gálvez, 116; Carlos E. Castañeda, Our Catholic Heritage in Texas, 1519-1936, 7 vols., 2: 311-48; Herbert E. Bolton, Texas in the Middle Eighteenth Century: Studies in Spanish Colonial History and Administration, 14-41, 53-54, 179-83.

CHAPTER II

TIMES OF TROUBLE: RISE OF THE
TEPEHUAN AND TARAHUMARA BARRIER

The time period, beginning with the Zacatecas silver strike in 1546 and closing with the Tarahumara revolts of the seventeenth century, held much greater significance for Indian resistance than is often implied. During this period, the border would be adjusted northward, putting its frontier pobladores into meaningful contact with the Indian people of its vastly enlarged northern territory. The basic Hapsburg policies towards these Indians, and the channels for their application, endured without fundamental changes until the Bourbons came to power in the eighteenth century. Sometimes amicable, sometimes hostile, Spanish relations with an Indian population that resisted convenient classification as friend or foe suffered from ambiguity. Spain's policy makers met and struggled with a new kind of enemy that had mastered the geographical conditions of a semi-arid, enormous expanse of land, especially the Tarahumara Indians.

In the late 1540s, the Zacatecas silver boom prompted a rush of miners, merchants, and ranchers northward. As Spaniards and their Mexican allies penetrated the land of the Chichimecas, the pressures from this cultural contact began fifty years of retaliatory Indian raids, characterized by military offensives that deterred effective northern settlement for several years.[1] Chichimeca country, bordered by an imaginary line along the northern Mexican states of Querétaro and Hidalgo, was a shifting cultural entity, not correspondent with well-defined geographical features. The nomadic Chichimecas, actually ten separate Indian nations, included the Guamares, Pames, Zacatecos, and Guachichiles (the four largest groups). The Spanish considered them strong adversaries, and during this era of frontier warfare, Hapsburg authorities in Mexico City formulated a policy for dealing with the northern tribes.[2]

Deeply frustrated by the futility of trying to secure the vast silver frontier against a shadow enemy, the government in Mexico City took a hard view of the Indian rebels. The southward flow of silver required protection, and the recently settled frontier area producing the silver needed defense against Chichimeca raiders. So, in the 1550s, Viceroy Luis de Velasco organized exploration parties for frontier expansion and settlement, and established militia, garrisoned towns to check hit-and-run attacks. He issued special regulations to protect traffic on the Mexico-Zacatecas silver highway (officially called the Camino Real de la Tierra Adentro or the Royal Inland Highway), ordered punitive campaigns against the Chichimecas, and granted special commissions and privileges to indios amigos (Indian auxiliaries) for their services against the Chichimecas.[3]

Of the major frontier policies, exploration and resettlement were fully implemented during Velasco's tenure, especially as this policy found expression in the northern exploration of Francisco de Ibarra on the farthest edges of the silver frontier. Other methods of quelling Indian disturbances proved ineffective, except for the use of Indian auxiliaries. "There seemed little doubt," observed Pedro Ahumada de Sámano, an adventurer-settler-miner of frontier origin, that military offensives had proved ineffective. The Chichimecas, safe in their mountain strongholds, could attack, withdraw, regroup, and quickly strike again as often as they wished. While Ahumada attempted punitive operations around Zacatecas, the results often proved negligible. He claimed that, "in all of the wars with them, the Guachichiles and Zacatecos are the more militant--four of these warriors can easily handle a hundred Mexican Indians."4 Like many frontiersmen, Ahumada did not think highly of indios amigos. He, like some northerners, thought them to be "idle" and little inclined to extensive campaigning. However, many other officials and frontier pobladores (including Teodoro de Croix) believed they were of great value.5

Despite Ahumada's difficulties with indios amigos from the southern provinces, on May 26, 1570, a royal order issued by His Majesty himself instructed judges and magistrates of the Audiencia of Nueva Galicia to gather the Indians into villas "where they may live in a civilized manner and have their organized government,..."6 This and similar changes in Spanish efforts to surround Indian people with a new religion, culture, societal attitudes and customs went hand-in-hand with military efforts to pacify the Chichimeca frontier.

In 1580, after two decades of intensive resistance, the viceregal government ordered a guerra de fuego y a sangre against the Chichimeca rebels. This war against a total population, combatant and noncombatant alike, included destruction of food, shelter, clothing, and stock, plus seizure of any possessions possible, leaving the hapless victims destitute in a bare land to starve or surrender. Total war merely provoked Chichimeca warriors to further resist and retaliate. The appropriation of more money and troops worsened the situation by fostering the traffic of captured Indian slaves and misuse of military monies.7 The Chichimeca War dragged on for a decade, seemingly stalemated, with Indian warriors at times threatening the very existence of Zacatecas.

In 1585, Mexico's seventh viceroy, the Marqués de Villamanrique, arrived, and the tide of war turned. But these further changes resulted from a shift in viceregal policy from Mexico City rather than any intensification of the military effort. Villamanrique extensively reexamined total war as a policy, and determining it ineffective, abandoned it in favor of missionaries as tools for pacification. This particular policy of directed culture change made the missions a dominant frontier institution. Viceroy Villamanrique also made it harder on military efforts. He outlawed enslavement of war captives, persecuting those found guilty of engaging in the lucrative slave traffic. He eliminated a number of useless presidios, reduced the number of troops operating in the field, required stricter audits of military expenditures, and forbade unauthorized offensives against Chichimeca rebels. Within four years, Spanish policy of guerra de fuego y a sangre had moved from total war to a new modus operandi of Christian charity.

In spring of 1591, the new viceroy, Luis Velasco II, distributed more rations of food commodities throughout Nueva Galicia and the new province of Nueva Vizcaya. He also recruited some four hundred Tlaxcalan families into eight model towns within Chichimeca territory to help pacify these nomads, and sent Franciscan and Jesuit missionaries instead of troops into the north. But it took Velasco's successor, the Conde de Monterrey, to completely alter the Indian policy that led to political consensus in exploiting Indian peoples. Luis Velasco II attracted Indians to mission life, speeding efforts to reduce the hostile to a peaceful and sedentary life.[8] By settling peaceful Chichimeca tribesmen in or near towns or formal religious communities, missionaries could instruct them in the Christian faith and reorganize their communities. It was expected that in time settlement would fill in, and civil government and secular clergy supplant the mission fathers who would then move beyond to establish new frontiers. In practice, Indians exploited this Royal policy as much as the Spaniards had a mind to enforce it.

Thus, as the northern frontier expanded, missionary fathers began the advance of Christian conversion and the imposition of cultural changes in all aspects of Indian society. From the beginning, Franciscans, Dominicans, Augustinians, and the Society of Jesus operated mission fields in New Spain that reduced or congregated Indian people into separate villages for the purposes of directed cultural change. In short, the mission would serve Church and State by converting Indians and in "civilizing" frontier areas, serving as a transitional institution between conquest and colonization.

In the 1590s, however, a pattern of resistance developed in the arroyo-scarred sierras of Nueva Vizcaya. The Acaxees, a small band people, in the high Sierra Madres revolted in 1601 and again in 1611. Missionary efforts among the Xiximes and Tepehuanes of the same province created divisions between the two bands. Apparently taking advantage of this division, in 1616 the Tepehuanes--aided by neighboring Acaxees, Conchos, Chinipas, Salineros, Tarahumaras, Tobosos, and Xiximes--rose in revolt. Unlike the Chichimeca rebellions of the 1540s and 1550s when the Guamares, Pames, Zacatecos, and Guachichiles took the offensive, the smaller band peoples of the north took to the use of fortified positions and hit-and-run campaigning in peripheral areas of Spanish control. As a tactic, however, it worked to their disadvantage--best exemplified by the Tepehuán rebellion of 1616. At that time, Tepehúan leaders, Quautlatas and Cogoxito, enlisted Indian alliances widely, attempting to show the Spaniards that a widespread network of resistance existed in northern New Spain -- a network facilitated in this case by a common enemy. In Sonora, Captain Diego de Hurdaide, fearing that the Tepehúan Revolt would spread southward, mobilized several citizen militias and presidio units against Nuri, Yecora, and Sinaloa allies of the Tepehúan.[9] Many band peoples, however, wanted no part of national alliance.

The Tepehuán Revolt is outstanding in its effective use of military organization and offensive tactics against the king's law and the king's officials. In November of 1616, religious leader Quautlatas organized an offensive that killed more than four hundred Spanish sympathizers, sending the surviving pobladores, miners, missionaries, and Indians fleeing to the protection of Sinaloa garrisons. Joined by a hechicero leader of great personal stature, Cogoxito, Quautlatas, turned his movement into a religious crusade, seeking to wipe out all vestiges of Spanish influence. His followers destroyed mission buildings, ranches, farms, and mines. With this initial success, the Acaxee, Chinipas and Tarahumaras were still not completely drawn into the rebellion. Cogoxito sought other support, sending four of his lieutenants to seek alliances with the Pima-speaking people of Sonora. The alliance seems to have been unfavorably transacted, for Sonora Indians did not participate in the war.

The Tepehuán revolt had a major cause. Quautlatas led a religious movement, a movement that influenced later Indian resistance in the Provincias Internas del Norte. To foster rebellion Quautlatas sponsored a holy image which spoke as revivalistic prophet. The hechicero proclaimed that "the people" should not accept the Spaniards' gods, but should return to the old ways, which could only occur if all the Spaniards and their Mexican allies were driven from their land. If done, no Spaniard would even return to oppress them. The hechicero promised that anyone who died while fighting the Spaniards would be brought back to life again. This highly emotional evangelistic movement had but a localized impact. Quautlatas himself promising that he would personally destroy such sacrilegious images as the blessed mother in the mission church of Zape.10 In short, a number of Indian people were persuaded to renew the old religious practices, but the majority stayed away from open resistance.11

After the Spaniards regrouped, presidials from Sinaloa and militia organized by Governor Gaspar de Alvear of Nueva Vizcaya mounted a major counteroffensive against the Tepehuanes. By 1617, after three punitive expeditions into Tepehuán territory, Quautlatas and the hechicero Cogoxito were killed as the rebellion turned to a weak conspiracy of hit-and-run raiding that exerted pressures on frontier peoples. The resistance dragged on for another year, with the Tarahumaras of Nueva Vizcaya terrorizing the harried pobladores.

Overextension of mission efforts appear to have sparked the rebellion. At the early mission of San Pablo Ballesa, founded by Jesuit Father Juan Fonte, the charge of Indian witchcraft and black magic continually surfaced. Also, because silver lodes were discovered in the San Pablo Valley, Father Fonte and his assistants moved much too quickly in trying to permanently settle the Tepehuanes into religious missions. The Tepehuán resisted the mounting pressures for mission life. They were a ranchería people, accustomed to a semi-nomadic culture. The Tepehuán moved their settlements seasonally from cultivated areas on high ground in the summer to protected canyons in the winter. Therefore, acceptance of mission life, meant not only replacement of their spiritual beliefs but also a complete reorganization of their culture. Under the leadership of a powerful shaman, they chose to rebel.

Mining activity can also be implicated in causing the Tepehuán Revolt. Discoveries of massive silver lodes at Santa Bárbara forced such a rapid frontier advance that the missionaries were caught defending their mission jurisdiction when local mine owners tried to recruit unauthorized allotments of workers from the missions. This open defiance of the mission fathers apparently encouraged the Tepehuán to disrespect Jesuit authority and credibility and thus contributed to the rebellion.12

After the Tepehuán Revolt, the Cabeza, Manite, Salinero, and Julime band peoples began to harass the frontier with hit-and-run raids. The Tarahumara revolts came in 1648, 1650, 1652, 1689, and 1697 with Toboso and Salinero participation in 1648. The Tarahumaras were not suppressed and throughout the seventeenth and eighteenth centuries the north continued to be threatened by renegade bands of Indians out of the Bolsón de Mapimí. There, Tobosos, Tarahumaras, and Conchos maintained continuous guerrilla warfare until depleted in ranks by death and disease. Yet this war of unconventional hit-and-run tactics would have far reaching historical consequences.

Warfare between the Indians and frontiersmen in seventeenth century Nueva Vizcaya saw a growth in the military prowess of Indian warriors and a disintegrating military potential on the part of Spanish frontier society. Various factors account for changing fortunes of the northern presidial, militiamen, or Indian auxiliary, but whatever the variables, warriors like the Tarahumara, maintained an overwhelming numerical advantage over their enemy. Given this situation, how could a struggling frontier population manage to maintain its existence?

Apparently, the very circumstances which made it impossible for the frontier military effort to prevent Indian uprisings seemed also to have prevented the Indians from expelling their enemy. This condition was basic to Indian culture, characterized by a great degree of ranchería individualism and, to a degree, tribal factionalism. Presidial companies, in many cases, discovered only small bands against which they could command their forces in an effort to conclude Indian resistance. In the 1640s, for example, Governor Diego Guajardo Fajardo pointed out four Indian caciques as rebel leaders, but not one represented the entire nation; hence, it seems that Indian leaders were never able, even should they have desired, to mobilize their entire potential against the frontiersmen.[13] It appears that Indian rebels were mostly engaged in limited raids across the rugged mountain region or sporadic but well-executed offensives.

A major cause of this impasse was the Tarahumara, Concho, and Toboso ability in frontier warfare. From the time of their first organized revolt in 1648, the warriors steadily developed defensive warfare, augmented by hit-and-run tactics. By February of 1693, Field Marshal Joseph Francisco Marín, after visiting most of the presidios of the province, explained that so numerous were the Indian nations of the north that they "make their expeditions through so many and diverse districts and with such swiftness and cunning that it is impossible for even a large number of soldiers to prevent such robberies and invasions."[14] Because they took an active military strategy of resistance, the Tarahumara people--even if factionalized and dispersed--demonstrated flexibility and ingenuity in the changing circumstances surrounding them. Their military power struggle with the Spanish "absorbing" world fostered a sense of autonomy.

The irony of the frontier impasse is Field Marshal Marin's statement that the Tarahumara, "who are now highly Hispanicized, have some degree of culture, and greatly apply themselves to the raising of cattle and the cultivation of their lands".[15] From the beginning of their contact with the outside world, Tarahumaras accepted Hispanicization voluntarily and from this position they obtained for themselves the best available barrier against the pressures that Spanish society applied against them. Not only did Field Marshal Marín speak to their economic and cultural development, but the mission fathers personally guarded them against rapacious Spaniards, and Mexicans. Had the Tarahumaras not played this game, it is doubtful whether they could have held off "forces" of the outside world.

It was not only through acquiescence to the demands of secular society that the Indians enhanced their strategies for survival, other facets of cultural resistance also raised their individual capacity to confront outside pressures in their homeland. The autonomous Indian rebels relied on traditional strategy. Indian warriors who attacked the hacienda of Salto de Agua and its church in 1648, used primarily pre-Spanish weapons. These consisted of pikes, arrows, and clubs. The pikes, though not as strong as their Spanish counterparts, were formidable. A contemporary Jesuit chronicler, José Pascual, believed that the bows were larger than those used in other parts of America; the arrows, though, were comparably short and were usually tipped with a poisonous material. Used less frequently were the clubs, shaped roughly like a baseball bat, only with a larger cross section at the tip.[16] The Tarahumara made few military concessions in this area of resistance.

In the Tarahumara revolt of 1652, led by the cacique, don Gabriel Teporame (sometimes called Teporaca), the Indian attacks displayed heroic valor, but their superior numbers were neutralized by the frontier soldiers' use of horses, musket, and above all, adaptation to a strange, eerie sort of enemy. But, by 1690, the Indians went back to a standard tactic. Instead of attacking in force, the war leaders formed their followers into "flying" squads. These squads attacked mestizo settlements and fought until forced to break and run. The squads were at once replaced by others which in turn were replaced by yet a third group. Thus, through sheer deployment of numbers, and despite heavy losses, the Indians literally overwhelmed the enemy. If, however, Indian warriors found themselves trapped by the enemy, the older men would stay and fight while the younger ones attempted to escape.

By 1690, the fourth Tarahumara rebellion manifested a semblance of alliance. The Tarahumara, aided by Concho, Toboso, and Jova renegades, joined forces and attacked Captain Juan Fernández de Retena's militia and Tepehuán allies at the mission of Papigochic. The attack was led by a Tarahumara hechicero who had convinced his followers through magic that he had corrupted and made useless the enemies gunpowder, "and if any warrior fell, by the sword or lance, he would arise within three days, safe and sound."[17] The loosely disciplined militia forces were fortunate, however, for the hechicero was killed in the first wave of the attack, and his followers fled to a fortified position. Subsequently, Captain Retana laid siege to the area and admitted some of the Indians to peace, as his predecessors had done, without properly subduing the enemy. As a result, this particular band of Indian warriors remained independent, and soon they were openly aiding the Jova, Concho, and Toboso people in defense of their own families or homeland.

By the late seventeenth century, hostile encounters increased. The settler-stockman Raphael de Ibarguen reports that between 1692-93, because a number of soldiers had been withdrawn from the presidios "by order of his Excellency for purposes of subjecting the province of New Mexico," he had the experience at his hacienda of having the enemy Indians take from him in just a few short months eight herds of mares, totaling 500 animals.[18] In carrying off the last ones, they killed on the summit of Don Pablo twelve vecinos, or Spanish colonists, and on that occasion other pobladores suffered the loss of many herds of horses and personal property.

Moreover, Ibarguen's twenty-six years of experience in the province of Nueva Vizcaya had convinced him that the entire multitude of rebellious Indians were involved in pilfering livestock and that a mobile strike force would not "suffice to keep them quite in the district where for the time being it might happen to be."[19] Consequently, it seems that the Tarahumara had gained a greater personal mobility and more control over their own lives; and, as the years passed, their raids were to increase in daring and intensity. By the end of the decade, thousands of animals stolen from the miners and pobladores of Nueva Vizcaya were driven northward, where a ready market was found.

After the initial shock, it appears that Indians lost their fear of firearms. Spanish soldiers or militia, grossly inaccurate in the aim and usually short of gunpowder, used their short supply of firearms whenever circumstances permitted. Despite this material and psychological advantage, when mounted units attacked Tarahumara fortifications, they often failed to dislodge the warriors. More often than not, reports Field Marshal Marín, military units found themselves besieged and forced to retreat through terrain "so extensive and the distance so great," that it was impossible "to effect a remedy for the hostilities and attacks which the Indians commit in so many and diverse localities, and perpetrate with expert art and cunning."[20]

Tarahumara methods of attacking northern travelers included the practice of ambushes and entrapments that rendered the horse useless. Field Marshal Marín had found during his inspection of frontier presidios that

> their first care is to strike down the horses. This, with the great skill that attends them in the use of such arms, they easily accomplish, and, being dismounted, the travellers are left defenseless and become the victims of their customary cruelties. If they perceive that they cannot make the attack without danger to themselves, they keep quiet-all of them, as is their custom, being painted and varnished the same color as the earth. . .[21]

Indian methods of fortification also included the practice of digging trenches and pits to entrap northern militia men. The success of this practice became evident in the Tarahumara uprising of 1690, which also gave evidence of the deterioration of frontier militia forces. In the following year, Governor Juan Isidro de Pardiñas, with a quickly organized militia force of two hundred soldiers and numerous Indian allies, was not even willing to attack Indian fortifications.[22] Instead, using a peace by purchase tactic, the governor spent much of his time granting pardons to Tarahumara rebels for past offenses, and investigating causes of the revolt. He was told by pardoned Indians that the rebellion had been planned for four years and that eleven nations had joined it, including the Pimas and Apaches. Governor Pardiñas remained at Yepómera for some time, and despite missionary opposition, sought implementation of amnesty and gift giving to avoid replay of this agonizing war.[23]

It appears that the Tarahumara cultivated allies among neighboring tribes, even among Indian settlements near and under surveillance of presidios, who would often give them advance warning of troop movements. These Indian or mestizo spies might be residents of mission villages or even caciques who for monetary reasons were friendly toward the hostiles. Tarahumara leaders gave such men presents, and spies were expected to vouch for the truth of any information. The Tarahumara dreaded traitors in their midst and tried to identify them so that they could be watched and killed when they became dangerous. Because they confronted a leakage of information, Tarahumara leaders seemed to be very circumspect about their own military plans; hence, they insisted that suspected traitors be closely watched.

On March 2, 1652, occurred another instance of Indian superiority in the siege of the Villa de Aguilar. Rebel leader Gabriel Teporame, also known as El Hachero (the hachet man), took up a position just beyond the range of the militia muskets, and there the Indians shouted insults and taunts in Spanish and in their native language at the encircled vaqueros, miners, and ranchers. Other warriors moved from farm to farm, now vacated by their frightened owners, and drove off the livestock without any resistance. Whatever the effectiveness of this tactical ploy, the Tarahumara, mounted such a strong offensive the following day that it effected the extinction of this frontier community for many years to come.[24]

In their revolts, the Indians were gathering increased quantities of military equipment, including coats of mail, swords, pikes, and leather jackets, as well as protective helmets. Most important, the animals which the Indians were taking were steadily increasing in number. For example, when the Jesuits evacuated the missions of Cahurichic and Tomochic in 1689, they left behind a large quantity of food, clothing, utensils, cattle, mission materials and horses. Within a short period, the plunder the Indians had captured enabled them to barter more effectively in the trade relations with band peoples of the north. This led Governor Gabriel del Castillo to complain a decade later that Apache and Pima nations constantly invading that province are putting it in extreme danger. The province had been depopulated by "the constant cruelties and devastation" of the enemy.[25] Looking at the whole context of Northern New Spain, the rebellions and guerrilla tactics of hit-and-run war served notice to Spain that the Indians wanted no part of their foreign influence.

Indian warriors had little fear of striking at the heart of Spanish society. In April of 1693, on the road from Parral to Santa Rosa de Cusihuiriachi, the merchant Andres de Jáurequi and six others were ambushed and killed by a band of Tarahumara warriors. Jáurequi himself was tied to a nearby tree and skinned alive. The new provincial governor, Gabriel del Castillo immediately issued orders for frontiersmen to retaliate inkind.[26] It appears that a cynical relationship of Indian attacks and settler retaliation had been firmly set into place, especially in or around the Royal Highway between major population centers.

Indian military success in their homeland was further enhanced by the nature of the frontier soldiery. Invariably, there was exceptionally low morale, lack of discipline, and military preparedness of troops that served His Majesty's frontier army. They were truly non-professionals born and raised on the northern frontier.

The presidials suffered great hardships and dangers, but they served well and effectively in this land of strife. The majority of the soldiery consisted of a sort of people's militia, who were born and raised on the frontier.

Maestro de Campo Marín in his 1693 report to Viceroy Conde de Galve stated that the men and their families were ill-clothed, ill-fed and ill-housed, or that they were the victims of exploitation by merchants, ranchers and their own officers. Competition among these people for a share of the soldiers' meager pay was high, but competitive price cutting was not a feature of the contest. Also, the presidio supply system in the more remote areas was particularly inadequate.[27] At times, rations were completely depleted, and soldiers were forced to forage for food in the nearby Indian settlements surrounding the presidio. If the Indians caught them stealing, they were often beaten or murdered. Financially, conditions were confusing, as illustrated by the account of Captain Agustín Herbante on the plight of presidio reductions:

> With respect to the saving which by these means is suggested to the most excellent señor viceroy there will be few who regard it desirable, although it appears that it may be done in another way, namely, in the agreement that the soldiers absolutely cannot take the field without a number of Indian friends, whose pay, sustenance, and the carriage of their provisions are charged to the real hacienda. There are very considerable expenses which might be avoided by ordering the captains of the said presidios to apply the pay of eight soldiers to keeping enlisted constantly the Indian friends that might be needed there. The number ought not go below forty, and they should be paid a salary of four pesos a month, which is quite sufficient, and with what else they get, they may be very well supported.[28]

In light of these problems, presidio captains met with Field Marshal Marín in the spring of 1693 recommending that the presidio system be reorganized and that large-scale offensive operations be mounted against the hostiles. Marín proposed that the way to carry on the war was namely, to leave at each presidio a dozen soldiers for defense and with "the rest to reconnoiter with squads of from forty to fifty(together with some friendly Indians, who are most successful as spies) the sites and locations of their habitations."[29]

Essentially defensive, the adapted plan sought to prevent the Indians, through a display of force, from mounting any major rising. As a strategy, however, it was ineffective. In the summer of 1697, Tarahumara leaders consolidated their forces into a general rebellion that for a time threatened to drive the frontiersmen out of the territory.

The northerners, then, became the victims of the summer campaign. As a strategy, the Indians executed it well. Field Marshal Marín did not overlook this problem; he responded accordingly in reporting that the most opportune time to wage war upon them was in the rainy season, as water could then easily be found for the soldiers and horses. The hardest and most difficult time was in the dry season, as all parts were then dry and sterile, and water could not be found except at great distances, hence the soldiery experienced suffering. "For this reason some of the men should be reserved (and they should be the least exhausted), in order to reconnoiter some localities and territory of the enemy at this time in order to thwart the expeditions which they are making into our territory."[30]

A more important reason for the success of summer campaigning is that it closely followed ranchería activity. Tarahumaras continued to maintain small fields within reach of the campaigning presidials, but they also planted larger crops far back in the mountain valleys where the soldiery feared to go. This suggests that the Indians continued planting the central valleys only as a trap designed to persuade the frontiersmen to continue their presidio defense system. Obviously, the Indians made summer campaigning of positive effect to themselves. As to the operations of the presidio, field-officers had been forced to keep people in the presidios, not drawing from them a single soldier to add to the flying company which the viceroy had placed in charge of Don Domingo Jiroinza, and, likewise, to ask the viceroy that members of the company should not be recruited from the citizenry of Parral.[31]

The truth is that the Tarahumara displayed an amazing ability to vanish before pursuing mobile companies of soldiers. Extreme ruggedness of their homeland, and the almost total lack of forage and water--which made the cavalry mounts almost useless--convinced frontier captains that this tribe could not be subjugated by just one, two or even three campaigns. Instead, presidials would have to undertake the task vigorously during all seasons. No period of rest could be allowed the rebels; they would have to be hounded and hunted from the mountain retreats and their fields and herds destroyed. Yet, the northerners were not in the military or economic position to implement guerra de fuego y a sangre. Frontier people were so poor, for example, that the Council of the Indies, governing institute for the American colonies, designated the geographical area as a "land of war," therefore, decreasing taxes while increasing royal subsidies.[32]

Several factors prevented the development of an overdose of total war. In the first place, the presidio proved to be unsatisfactory as a military institution. The troops were a mixed and restless lot, often of frontier origin, and despite repeated prohibitions, abandoned their monotonous assignments for the lure of new opportunities. Moreover, field-officers displayed a reluctance to participate in extended campaigns, especially if these were distant from their immediate area. Consequently, during the latter part of the seventeenth century, the burden of defense was shifted to citizen militias drawn from such populations as Durango, Santa Bárbara, and San José del Parral. Mixed-blood settlers eagerly sought the trappings of military service, such as uniforms, rank, and military honors, in order to perpetuate the military spirit of their ancestors, but they were disinclined to perpetuate the martial spirit of those same ancestors. Thus the training and effective command of volunteer companies required in turn a resident staff of officers and sergeants, whose duties, however, allowed them plenty of time to engage in mining, ranching, and commerce to supplement their meager and often irregular pay.[33]

The most effective reinforcements for the presidio system were indios amigos. The Indian service was composed of nomadic warriors serving as allies either independently or in concert with the citizen militia, but almost always under their own command. The auxiliaries were usually, but not always, drawn for temporary duty on a quota basis from established Indian communities near the presidios. There were some mission communities of the Tarahumara, Pima, and Opata villages regularly organized as military companies. Also, individual Indians were hired or impressed in to temporary service as scouts, guides, spies and interpreters. But the burden of defense still fell on the distinctive frontier soldiery. For this reason, Field Marshal Marín was of the opinion that it would have been fruitful and of far-reaching consequences to introduce and cultivate among the Indian nations discords and distrusts. Commander Marín believed that if disunity were created, then they would come to fear each other. Thus, those Indians already converted to mission-life may "be conserved and maintained through fear of those unreduced; while the latter may be coerced through the others, and whenever it might be convenient to wage war upon them with these latter ones. This is a most essential matter and great care ought to be taken to observe it and to follow a plan so advantageous."[34]

Such were the aspects of warfare in this northern region. It was a war that by the turn of the century found the Spanish settlers in these hostile lands facing a major problem. On the one hand, they did not have the troop strength to deal with Indian revolts in the northern region. On the other hand, much as Spanish residents suffered directly, they did not have the militia strength, time or organization to prevent Indian rebels from becoming stronger, to reinforce the presidio system, or to provide some replenishment for the soldiers. Therefore, as the seventeenth century continued, Indian attacks mounted, and there emerged a guerrilla warfare in the northern land broken only by concentrated "peace by purchase" efforts. This precarious situation was not to be more effectively controlled until consolidation of frontier policy by Bourbon authorities. In the late eighteenth century, General Jacobo Ugarte y Loyola offered several Indian bands a general amnesty, removed vagrants from their land, and handled criminal cases locally.[35] But this, by no means, put an end to Indian resistance.

LIPAN WARRIOR
Drawing by Arthur Schott, 1857 (W.H. Emory, <u>Report on the United States and Mexican Boundary Survey</u>, vol. 1, Washington, D.C., 1857).

CHAPTER II

FOOTNOTES

[1]Chichimeca warfare involved deception, concealment, intelligence, improvisation, surprise attacks and quick withdrawals, and above all, avoidance of open tests of strength with the Spaniards. The Indian warrior lacked the logistic capability and the time for unhindered preparation for so-called "conventional war."

[2]The principal authority on the Chichimeca conflict is Philip W. Powell, Soldiers, Indians, and Silver: The Northward Advance of New Spain, 1550-1600. See also his Mexico's Miguel Caldera, The Taming of America's First Frontier, 1548-1579.

[3]Against the Chichimecas, Indian allies generally included Tarascans from Michoacan country, Aztecs (the Mexica), Otomíes from Querétaro, or Cazcanes from villages north of Guadalajara.

[4]Información acerca de la rebelión de los indios zacatecos y guachichiles a pedimento de Pedro Ahumada Sámano, año de 1552, Colleccion de documentos para la historia de Hispano-America, 14 vols., 1: 262.

[5]Teodoro de Croix to José de Gálvez, No. 735, Informe General, Arizpe, April 23, 1782, paragraphs 48-50, AGI, Guadalajara 253.

[6]A copy of the Royal Order of 1570, communicated by the king, appears in Hackett, Historical Documents, 1: 101-03.

[7]R. Stafford Poole, "War by Fire and Blood," The Americas 22 (October 1965): 115-37.

[8]Powell, Soldiers, Indians, and Silver, 183-91.

[9]Relación enviada por el capitán Castañeda sobre el Alzamiento que intentaron los indios de la Vizcaya y de la paz que ha resultado despues de la guerra, 1604 (enclosed as eight folios), fol. 2, AGI, Guadalajara 7.

[10]Relación breve y sucinta de los sucesos que ha tenido la guerra de los Tepehuanes de la Nueva Vizcaya..., in Hackett, Historical Documents, 2: 100-13.

[11]Guillermo Porras Múñoz, La Frontera con los Indios de Nueva Vizcaya en el Siglo XVII, 194-195.

[12]María Teresa Huerta Preciado, Rebeliones indígenes en el Noreste, de Mexico el la época Colonial, 13-16.

[13]Spicer, Cycles of Conquest, 30-32.

[14]Joseph Francisco Marín to Viceroy Conde de Galve Parral, September 30, 1693, Hackett, Historical Documents, 2: 364-409.

[15]Ibid.

[16]Noticias de José Pascual, 1651, Documentos para la historia de Mexico, 21 vols. (Mexico, 1853-57), 3: 186.

[17]Peter Masten Dunne, Early Jesuit Missions in Tarahumara, 173.

[18]Raphael de Ibarguen to Joseph Francisco Marín, September 20, 1693, Hackett, Historical Documents, 2: 381-84.

[19]Ibid.

[20]Testimonio de cartas. . ., September 30, 1693, Hackett, Historical Documents, 2: 397.

[21]Ibid.

[22]Dunne, Early Jesuit Missions in Tarahumara, 169.

[23]Autos fos sobre las Ymbasiones que hacen los Indios rebeldes en este R.no Y los que se ban actuando sobre la guerra offensive que se les aze--por el s.r. Sarg. to M.or Don Juan Ysidro de pardiñas Villar de francos cav.o Del orden de Santiago Gov. or y Cap.n Gen.l deste R.no y provincias de la Nueva vizcaya por su Mg.d-1690, AGN, Provincias Internas 29, expediente 5.

[24]Porras Múñoz, La frontera con los Indios de Nueva Vizcaya, 199-203.

[25]Report of Governor Gabriel del Castillo, April 3, 1698, Hackett, Historical Documents, 2: 433.

[26]Gabriel del Castillo to Viceroy Conde Galve, Durango, May 2, 1693, Hackett, Historical Documents, 2: 304-306.

[27]Testimonio de cartas . . ., September 30, 1693, Hackett, Historical Documents, 2: 365-401.

[28]Don Agustín Herbante to the Maestro de Campo, September 12, 1693, Hackett, Historical Documents, 2: 375.

[29]Testimonio de cartas . . ., September 30, 1693, Hackett, Historical Documents, 2: 399-401.

[30]Ibid., 401-3.

[31]Respuesta fiscal sobre diferentes puntos de guerra con los indios enemigo de reyno del Parral . . ., 1 de abril, 1698, Hackett, Historical Documents, 2: 418-21.

[32]Consulta del Consejo de Indias, 1605, AGI, Mexico 270.

33Moorhead, The Presidio, 178-84, José Ignacio Gallegos, Durango colonial, 184-215.

34Testimonio de cartas . . ., September 30, 1693, Hackett, Historical Documents, 2: 403.

35Moorhead, The Apache Frontier, 129.

CHAPTER III

THE PUEBLO AND TARAHUMARA REVOLTS

Before the eighteenth century, at least on paper, Hapsburg Indian policy in the north was based on aggressive defense. Yet two problems remained to be confronted--frontier attitudes and proposed projects that simply complicated matters, and an increasingly dangerous situation created by Indian rebels in Nueva Vizcaya, Sinaloa, and Sonora. The crown considered these northwestern lands, dominated by Indian hostiles, to be in a state of siege. The silver strikes, farming or grazing lands (or so it was thought) were deterred from development on this Indian frontier. Although, the Gila River basin, Río Grande Valley, and Conchos River drainage supported irrigated farming, the king's peacemakers felt they held even these areas insecurely. In the far north, the Spanish presence did little more than disrupt the traditional struggle between nomadic and sedentary tribes. Also, the northern tribes, for the most part, knew and understood Spanish motives.

The Pueblo Revolt of 1680, another part of the chain reaction of rebellions, complicated international events in the north, and shocked Spain into reexamining its pacification program. Since its settlement in 1598, New Mexico had proved much too demanding on Spanish colonist, and Indian alike, and the Pueblo rebellion merely manifested a people's ultimate reaction against punitive Spanish policy towards the Indian leadership. Other revolts occurred on the northern frontier, but this was one of the larger and more violent. Led by charismatic Popé (Po-pay) and his lieutenants, the Pueblo Indians managed in this well-executed uprising to kill twenty-one of their Franciscan missionaries and an estimated three hundred eighty Spanish colonizers, sending the surviving two thousand Spaniards and Christian Indians fleeing down the Río Grande Valley to the El Paso area. The success of the militant action inspired the several nations to the south to continue their raiding, plundering, tactics of what has been called the Great Northern Revolt.[1]

The Pueblo Revolt had several causes. Problems with civil administration and policy over the distribution of labor prevailed. Several civil officials lacked integrity and, similarly, many religious and secular officials exploited and mistreated the Indians. However, the major problem lay in conflicting interests over labor rights between Church and State. The religious and civil programs operated somewhat independently. Franciscans sought to construct agricultural communities within Pueblo townsites, giving Indians both Christian teaching and horticulture techniques. Until 1630, there seemed to be little problem with the several royal authorities, but as the Franciscans began to build a surplus of commodities, prosper, and control the labor market, troubles quickly surfaced. In essence, governors were required to collect tribute for the king and, in addition, were privileged to engage in limited private trade. As a result, a struggle developed between the several vested interests for temporal affairs in Pueblo villages.

Further aggravating the New Mexico wide conflict, civil authorities tended to use their office for personal gain rather than creation of a Hispanicization policy advocated by the king. Several governors, for example, built a profitable business in hides, salt, woven goods, and agricultural products. Missionaries complained this lured Indians way from the mission teachings and even from their own mission industries. Likewise, governors charged that the missionaries forced Indians to work for them.2 This conflict both baffled and discouraged the Pueblos as secular and religious officials continued to battle for the next fifty years.

Governors such as Juan Antonio de Otermín and missionaries not only squabbled over the mission program. To further colonization efforts in New Mexico, His Majesty's vassals apparently confiscated Indian property and made them work without any pay. Father Nicolás López, a prominent religious of that period, asserted that employment of Pueblo Indians in labor drafts produced no tribute for the king, nor to the religious proprietor of the Indian community.3 In New Mexico, it was originally presumed that the colonizers would cultivate their own lands and employ Indians only at harvest time, but the Indians soon were used as household servants and labor in the struggling weaving or stockraising industry. Spanish policy in New Mexico, essentially a coercive policy, simply fostered economic exploitation and further added to the increasing pressures on Pueblo society.

The device compelling personal service from Indians went by various names. In New Spain, it was generally called repartimiento, and Indian obligated to serve in it termed indios de servicio. But the term repartimiento covers many things and calls for clearer definition. Its generic meaning is allotment or partition. Thus, when colonists held repartimientos of lands, it was confused with encomienda. Repartimiento also involved the practice of alcaldes mayores inducing Indians to purchase tools, seeds, and livestock from them on credit, the debts thus incurred becoming liens against Indian wages. Standard usage of repartimiento applied to allotment of Indians required for some specific tasks, but on the New Mexico frontier, Indians were generally under the supervisorial authority of the mission fathers.

The missionary procedure of convincing the Pueblos to serve king and empire also caused problems. Accomplished largely through the introduction of new crops, clothing, agricultural implements, food and colorful pageantry, Franciscan missionary work at first proceeded successfully. But around 1630, though Father Alonso de Benavides claimed the baptism of sixty thousand Pueblos, a major shortcoming became apparent--the Pueblos had not given in to the doctrinal education nor renounced their own religious ceremonies.4 Ceremonial dances, offering of prayer sticks, and Kiva society membership continued. Indian religion seemed as strong as ever. Additionally, several New Mexican governors appeared to tolerate and even encourage internal dissension among the Pueblos and their religious superiors.

In the 1650s, Governor Bernardo López de Mendizabal's secular/missionary relations led to a widening of the conflict in New Mexico. López stated publicly that he would tolerate Indian dances, appointed as head of one pueblo an Indian who had killed the previous friar, and gave other villages permission to perform their religious ceremonies. At a ceremony in his honor, he even encouraged participation by some of his soldiers in the dances. The Franciscans took this as opposition to their program, and in 1661, the Franciscan custodian decreed absolute prohibition of all Indian dances and instructed missionaries to seek out and destroy the evil Kachina masks, prayer feathers, and other religious images. In all, 1,600 masks and other items were destroyed. Such obliteration of their sacred tokens embittered the Pueblos, and their growing anger over continued encroachment on Indian society fueled a determination to no longer yield or compromise.

External conflict further aggravated the Spanish-Franciscan conflict in New Mexico. Instead of decreasing traditional intertribal warfare, Spanish occupation of the province caused considerable increase. Though Spanish residents joined in defending Pueblo lives and property, their growing settlements and the productive Indian villages provided attractive targets for nomadic warriors of the north, and raids by Apaches continued in intensity and daring. By mid-century, warfare with Apaches, usually attacking in small bands and on foot, increased so greatly that three southern pueblos had to be abandoned while the others remained constantly harassed. Pueblo fortified villages still thwarted the Apaches and Comanches since they had yet to acquire horses and firearms. New Mexicans, at this time, could only content themselves with punitive military campaigns that achieved little or nothing in their lands east, north, and west of New Mexico.

The whipping of Indian leaders sparked the revolt. In 1675, Governor Juan Francisco Treviño heard from an Indian informer of a group of Indian shamans gathering at one of the northern pueblos. A raid by the governor's soldiers netted forty-seven Indians who were immediately accused of witchcraft and promotion of idolatry. The governor had three of them executed, a fourth committed suicide, and the rest received severe lashings and admonishment before their release. Among them was Popé, the San Juan hechicero, who would harbor a contempt for white men and plans for revenge.[5]

As a result of the punishment, people of the several Indian villages determined to act against this often used form of oppression. A few small rebellions staged in the past to test the strength of Spanish forces taught the Indians that only a united effort would defeat them. However, such unity was foreign to Pueblo culture since, each village being an independent political unit, little interaction occurred, except ceremonially among members of the various religious organizations. But Popé held an important office in one of these religious fraternities which enabled him to coordinate secret meetings, enlist the aid and cooperation of Alonso Catití, Luis Tapatú, and other Pueblo leaders, and formulate strategy for revolt. His final plans were simple: on the morning of August 11, 1680, rise up and kill all missionaries and settlers. When news of the revolt leaked out, he re-scheduled it for a day earlier. Many of the pobladores, luckily alerted, managed to escape before being killed.[6]

The Pueblo Revolt is representative of northern intertribal organization for the purposes of eliminating the Spanish presence in New Mexico. Every village north of Isleta Pueblo joined in this widespread uprising and campaign directed by capable Indian leadership born of secular efforts to discipline a group of ceremonial officials.[7] The Indians allowing the survivors to escape indicates the major objectives of the revolt: elimination of the Spaniards and, if possible, total expulsion of all their cultural baggage. Spanish military weakness offered a seemingly unusual opportunity, and the Pueblos thus permitted the refugees' flight southward. Some of the Christian Indian refugees took temporary shelter at the community of Isleta, while Spaniards, mestizos and castas moved on to El Paso. Though they remained there some twelve years, and made a few feeble efforts to punish the Pueblos, no effective attempt at reconquest occurred until 1692.

During the revolt, the Pueblos burned or otherwise destroyed ranches, farms, and mission buildings as well as church records and furnishings. Testimony given by Pueblo Indians, Juan and Francisco Lorenzo in December of 1681, captured in Governor Antonio de Otermín's abortive reconquest attempt of 1681, indicates that Popé and his subordinates wanted to obliterate all traces of Spanish society. Juan and Francisco Lorenzo, brothers from San Felipe Pueblo, testified before Maestre de campo Juan Domínguez de Mendoza that Popé and several of his lieutenants came to their pueblo, ordering the churches burned and the holy images broken and destroyed. The leaders seized everything in the sacristy, saying they had wearied of serving the missionaries.[8] Yet a few months later, the Pueblo Indians had deposed Popé for his own autocratic rule. In his place, they elected Luis Tapatú of Picuris, captain and right hand man to Popé.

Mestizos from the south and castas joined the Pueblos in their revolt, remaining in New Mexico after the colonists fled. Some mixed-bloods played leading roles in the rebellion. Alonso Catití, coordinator of the southern pueblos in the uprising, was a mestizo, and the mixed-blood, Francisco, commonly called El Ollita, was part Indian and part casta. Governor Otermín noted that many mestizos, who were skillful on horseback and who could manage firearms as well as any soldier, followed the Pueblos into rebellion. Indeed, "these persons incited them to disobedience and boldness in excess of their natural iniquity. . . ."[9]

Many castas sympathized with the Pueblos, and some even courageously joined in the rebellion. Yet some Indians changed sides, especially within the Indian leadership. Bartolome de Ojeda, a Zía who fought well during the revolt, joined the survivors in El Paso and became a valuable guide when they planned the reconquest. Captain Luis Tapatú and his brother Lorenzo went over to the Spaniards, Domingo Romero from Tesuque, and Don Felipe from Pecos also joined the Spanish side of this struggle. Governor Otermíns' counteroffensive of late 1681 contained an Indian component of twenty Mansos, fifty-four Piros, thirty Tiwas, and eight Jemez amigos.[10]

By 1684, Indian rebels had spread news of the successful Pueblo Revolt into Nueva Vizcaya, Sinaloa, and Sonora. Attempting to coordinate a massive uprising, they inspired Janos, Sumas, and Mansos in the El Paso area to rebel, and as sedition continued, Tobosos, Conchos, and Julimes took heart and joined in. South of Casas Grandes, Suma and Concho warriors destroyed mission centers and killed several whites, while Tobosos attacked the presidio of Cerro Gordo, wounded many of its defenders, and ran off with the horses. These uprising ended in the destruction of nine missions and two Spanish settlements. Meanwhile, Indian renegades from the Bolsón de Mapimí increasingly took to the warpath in and around San José de Parral and Santa Bárbara, and soon were joined by Seri, Pima, Opata and other Sonoran allies who had rebelled on and off since 1650. As news of the Pueblo success spread, the Tarahumara leadership of Nueva Vizcaya conspired a massive uprising for the late 1680s. It was in this untimely environment that the seven missionaries who served some five thousand Tarahumara and one hundred frontiersmen living in thirty-two pueblos in the highlands of Tarahumara started a serious penetration into their northern strongholds.

That relations between the Tarahumara and the crown's religious men were not good had already been indicated, and the suggestion has been made that Pueblo success stimulated greater resistance. But by 1684, overall relations appear to have deteriorated even further. Silver strikes of importance were discovered at Coyachic, just a few miles northeast of Cusihuiriachic. Later, another lode was discovered near the mission of San Bernabé. Just as the Pueblo Indians were exploited, so now was the Tarahumara countryside overwhelmed by missionaries, merchants, and hacendados. It does not seem unreasonable to suppose, then, that by 1689, the new governor of Nueva Vizcaya, Don Isidor de Pardiñas (1687-1693), member of a noble family of Galicia, fearful of a revolt and missionary involvement, was determined to keep a stricter audit on church-state affairs. As in New Mexico, the missionaries, by disturbing the Indian labor force, by providing potential centers of agitation against the government, and by establishing claims to land which might be needed in the course of economic development, interfered with what some local officials considered to be the most efficient way of dealing with Indians.

Thus, Governor Pardiñas's sudden offensive against the Society of Jesus weakened their benign paternalism in the eyes of the Indian leadership. Like New Mexico, the religious and civil society of Nueva Vizcaya contained many potentialities for strife. Conflicts between ecclesiastical and political authorities were common. Civil officials sought to take Tarahumaras as laborers, to violate and abuse them, to destroy their religious articles, to exact extralegal tribute from them, and to profit from them in other ways. Miners, Spanish landowners, and vecinos were always alert to the possibilities of kidnapping women and children and selling them into slavery. Conflict with the presidio soldiers was also frequent. But the Pardiñas and following administration of Gabriel del Castillo, repeatedly criticizing the Society of Jesus for their severity with the Indians, their supposed exploitation of Indian labor, and their moral behavior, compares closely to events leading up to the Pueblo Revolt.

At issue for the Tarahumara, similar to Pueblo Indian issues, was restoration of a respect for religious life, village autonomy, and collective economic development. Indian leaders apparently believed that the human rights long enjoyed by the Tarahumara people were being routinely violated by the Spaniards, especially by Spanish society, the practice of their own internal government, illegal and unjust punitive campaigning against them, and the whipping or imprisonment of Tarahumara leaders. Also, like the Pueblo grievances, drought, famine, and disease had caused a tremendous imbalance in the Tarahumara way of life. Clearly, the grievances are similar. As might have been expected, in late November of 1689, in a sudden and devastating move, Ignacio Osebaca, governor of

Cocomórachic, put together an uprising that involved seven other Indian leaders. Elements in Osebaca's following were represented largely by individual or small group attachments to him and his lieutenants. Typical of Osebaca's lieutenants, and one who was said to be a relative, was the hechicero Tepuraca. Unlike Osebaca, whose contact with the Jesuits is something of a puzzle, Tepuraca never converted to Christianity and continually adhered to traditional Tarahumara teachings. Another lieutenant was Chigoynare, Governor of Nahuerachic, and a close friend of Osebaca. Still a third conspirator was Sopequemec Norá, who was part Concho, and who helped to ally the Concho and Jova in the conspiracy. These figures, and others like them, largely represented the limit of Osebaca's influence on direct tribal representation; yet with the aid of his persuasion, these seven individuals, who did not have leading positions in the traditional administrative sense, were able to mobilize highland people from most of the missions.[11]

In the long run, like the Pueblos, the revolt was a failure. In April of 1690, Indian warriors broke up into squads and attacked Yepómera in northwestern Tarahumara. On the first Tuesday after Easter, they descended at daybreak upon the home of Father Foronda, a member of the Society of Jesus, and killed him and two Spanish laymen who were staying with him. Then, allied with the Toboso, Concho, Guazapar, and Jova, they attacked the church sites of Temosachic, Nahuerachi, and Sirupa. Fathers Wilhelm Illink and George Hostinsky, both Bohemians new to the missions of Cahurichic and Tomochic, were forced to flee as their two mission dwellings were also destroyed. Governor Pardiñas at Parral, hearing of the insurrection, sent Captain Juan Fernández de Retana with fifty soldiers and two hundred Indian allies into the countryside. Retana's forces entered the territory and was immediately attacked, but in the early fighting, Ignacio Osebaca was killed and his followers quickly dispersed. Later, Governor Pardiñas came up with a force of two hundred soldiers and three hundred Indian allies, but the Tarahumara had vanished into the inaccessible mountains. Pardiñas then marched unmolested to Yepómera, pitched camp, and busied himself in creating a deeper gulf between himself and the Jesuits, by issuing a general pardon to the conspirators. Thus, as quickly as it had began, ended the conspiracy and revolt of 1689.[12]

A remarkable feature of the conspiracy was the support for it which came from northern tribes. It is true that the actual insurrection misfired, but that it existed at all, that other tribal leaders actually took part in Osebaca's planning, is a demonstration of the difference between it and the Pueblo conspiracy of 1680. Some of the outside support may be looked upon as a tactical alliance against the Spaniards and their allies, since the Tarahumara had known tactical alliances in the past. Yet, this does not explain the reason for Sopequemec Norá in Osebaca's following, and his motives are not explained by the sheltering adjective detribalized-- a term which creates as many difficulties as it solves. It would appear that consequences of the Pueblo Revolt had greatly influenced the Tarahumara leadership as to the greater value of confederation, and that they were prepared to seek openly a northern alliance.

No sooner was the rebellion effectively over, and the leaders and their sympathizers well in hand, than rumor began to circulate of another conspiracy. The new governor, Gabriel del Castillo (1693-1698), received the information that a number of hechiceros were meeting at one of the northern missions. By April 1696, Father Joseph Neumann, newly appointed official visitador and no great admirer of the governor, reported that the conspiracy had spread throughout his mission district and he requested that Castillo send a force of troops into the province. In response to Neumann's suspicions, Governor Castillo ordered Captain Juan Fernández de Retana with fifty soldiers and two hundred Indian allies up the Río Conchos and into Papigochic country, where he interrogated suspected Tarahumara rebels.[13] It was natural that any person who had been in any way connected with the previous revolt should fall under suspicion. Therefore, proceeding further northwest to Yepómera, center of the former uprising, Captain Retana conducted another punitive campaign against Indian leaders who did not fit into the pattern of conduct acceptable to the Spaniards. These measures, however, were unsuccessful, for at Cocomórachic, Tarahumara people fled and reassembled in a stronghold overlooking the valley of Sirupa, rather than face the humilation of imprisonment. There, they waited Captain Retana's arrival and continuation of the 1689 uprising.[14]

Motives of this particular uprising were the same as the Pueblo Revolt. The Tarahumara could no longer tolerate the sharply defined political conflict between Spaniards and Jesuits, the economic pressures of Spanish miners, hacendados, and merchants, and the military campaigns against them was greatly weakening Indian morale and numbers. As a consequence, the Tarahumara Indians revolted.

Informed of their defection at Cocomórachic and sure that he was headed for trouble, Retana, recently promoted to general, laid siege to the mesa stronghold while he sent for reinforcements. But the Tarahumara waited until nightfall, then stole away, leaving their livestock behind as a ploy. General Retana then ordered his indios amigos out to scout the countryside for the rebels. Sixty were captured, and in late March 1697, thirty were shot and decapitated, their impaled heads lining the highway to Yepómera to serve as a warning to all potential conspirators. The remaining captives were than taken to Matachic, where the same psychological weapon was employed against the Indians of this mission.

News of this event shook the frontier, and Spanish confidence that these summary executions intimidated incipient rebels was wishful thinking. At Tomochic, four hundred Tarahumara rebels allied with two hundred Jovas and Tobosos, sacked and burned the mission site. The following day, the mission of Mesachic was also sacked, with the resident Jesuit George Hostinsky having to flee for his life. Local officials had thus miscalculated; before the month was out, seven mission sites were in ruins with the insurrections spreading to the missions of Sonora. Then, several mission caciques of the northern Tarahumara countryside enthusiastically followed the scheme of charismatic Concho leader, Puziligi, to strike over the entire northern frontier in a surprise attack. No quarter was to be given to any Spaniard but, unlike the Pueblo conspiracy, the Society of Jesus would be spared.[15]

By June 1697, with their numbers now increased to over one thousand, the insurgents ranged beyond Papigochic and attacked Echoquita in Joseph Neumann's district. Another war party then attacked Neumann's own mission site of Sisoguichic. Here, General Retana met the warriors and dispersed them after taking heavy losses. The battle cost him fifteen wounded and five dead. But it was a turning point. The Tarahumara retreated to their mountain fortifications and resumed irregular warfare. Puzilegi and other Concho rebels were captured and put to death while their families were exiled. The revolt dragged on in Sinaloa and Sonora, where the alliance destroyed several mines and settlements. But after 1698, the movement northward was characterized by small raids on isolated haciendas, ranches, supply caravans, and mission sites.

It was obvious from this climate of suspicion that, if the work of the missionaries were not to be impeded, mission fathers would have to produce some clear evidence that their missions had not been centers of religious sedition. For several months after the rebellion, mission fathers apparently indulged in an outpouring of communications to government officials and co-workers in the field. In the end, they did not quiet rumors that Jesuits were responsible for the revolts, and the political conflicts in Nueva Vizcaya continued. They did, however, convince the new governor, Juan Bautista de Larrea, that he should leave one mobile company in Tarahumara country. Governor de Larrea also relocated suspected rebels in more populous centers of loyal Indians, made a round of visitations to the various mission districts, whipped and executed prime movers in the fourth Tarahumara rebellion, and exiled other suspected troublemakers.

If an indirect approach is taken regarding why the Pueblo and Tarahumara revolts failed to achieve their aims and were brought under control, their significance in wider northern New Spain may emerge. First of all, leaders and their immediate adherents seemed to be "marginal men" caught between the Indian way of life and the social integration they confronted, which offered opportunities at the cost of accepting frightening risks. They were, as the Pueblos' Popé confused in their aims; they wanted both to destroy and to preserve; to stage both a demonstration and a revolution; to assert a traditional dignity by martyrdom; and, by the same token, to mold a new Indian community. The ambivalence of their aims was reflected in their organization with its mixture of short-range and long-range elements. Their very position on the bridge of transition between ways of life which had neither traditions nor prospects in common was responsible for their failure to understand the type of movement which, in a frustrated and incoherent way, they were creating. The local Spanish government, though slow to realize what was being created around the missions, was well qualified to identify what had happened when the movements passed from the stage of conspiracy to that of insurrection. The administration had at its disposal the vast legacy of the colonial experience in central Mexico and the Chichimecas, while the disproportion in physical resources between the Indians, their invaders, made its success in repressing revolts almost inevitable.

The military, on the other hand, was clearly aware that it had at last met not simply tribal revolt against alien rule, but an organized movement aimed at creation of what the Hapsburgs had foreseen with apprehension--a northern unity in opposition to Spanish paternalism that transcended the tribal and other divisions of the subject people. It was this encompassing intertribal aspiration of Osebaca's movement, however, which, as much anything, caused it to fail, for in 1689, the majority of Tarahumaras were tribesmen first and foremost, disinclined to abandon customary associations and subordinations. And among those Tarahumara people Christianized to some extent by the Jesuits, most found security in attachment to a Jesuit hegemony that was unquestionably endowed with power and prestige, rather than by participating in the fortunes of local hechiceros.

Many Indian people who agreed substantially with Popé's or Osebaca's grievances, and others who admired their achievement in appropriating so much detailed knowledge of Spanish strengths and weaknesses, were not prepared to be carried into armed resistance against all that they had come to regard with hatred-- their resistance stopped short of attacking the front-line persuaders of peace. To rebel was not only to profess ability to handle the new complexities of cash economy and wide territorial and national relations, but also to raise the spectra immediate conflict with an alien power that had, within living memory, imposed its system on tribal elders. That Osebaca and Popé were able to inspire a measure of "spiritual" unity among adherents of different tribes was one of the most significant features of their achievement. But that measure of unity had neither the strength nor the range to arm them adequately against what has so correctly been called "the culture of conquest."[16]

Should the revolts and Osebaca's or Popé's quick demise be viewed as futile and pathetic efforts doomed to defeat, productive of no other result than the inevitable ensuing despotism? Should they merely be qualified as an outburst counting for little when weighed against the achievements of Indian warfare in a later century? These questions, however compelling, must be stated in other terms: What could northern Indian rebels have accomplished had they lacked an insurrectionary spirit and the king's vassals not come to fear and respect them?

No matter, in 1685, Robert Cavelier, Sieur de la Salle, eyeing possible expansion of French commerce with a chain of trading posts from the St. Lawrence and Mississippi River systems, planted his ill-fated colony at Matagorda Bay on the Texas coast. Fear of such French incursion and its inherent threat to the northern provinces of New Spain provoked another era of Spanish military preparedness. By 1690, a few missionaries, supported by soldiers, established themselves in Texas, but Apaches and Caddoans from the north (the so-called Nations of the North) soon drove them out. Of the some twenty-five Caddo groups, loosely leagued in one of three confederacies, the Hasinai was the largest and occupied the upper reaches of the Neches and Angelina rivers in East Texas. The first Caddoans to encounter Spaniards and their allies, they gave the Texas settlements the most trouble. The other two confederacies were the Kadohadacho, near Big Bend region of the Red River in northeast Texas, and the Natchitoches, located downstream from them on the Red River. Two independent Caddoan groups included the Adaes, north of the Natchitoches in the Red River Valley, and the Hais, situated in the area of present San Augustine, Texas.[17]

With the Bourbons encouraging frontier development, the Spanish established a strategic operational base for eventual reoccupation of Texas on the south bank of the Rio Grande. Although northern Indian resistance deterred effective settlement until 1716, the short-lived presidio of Nuestra Señora de los Dolores, near the Neches River in the northeastern part of the province, was founded, followed in 1718 by the more important and permanent presidio settlement of San Antonio in south central Texas. In 1772, the presidio of La Bahía near the shore of Matagorda Bay, developed into Bourbon jurisdiction over temporal affairs in the northern provinces.

Spain occupied Texas for exclusively defensive reasons. Though the French threat in Texas disintegrated before Spaniards could confront it militarily, Texas remained a beleaguered province. Far from the center of viceregal power in Mexico City, the territory's vastness mitigated against effective defense by the presidio system and held no incentive for any appreciable immigration. These circumstances forecast the precarious foothold in Texas that Spain eventually abandoned east of the Rio Grande. Economically, Bourbon officials attempted a legitimate commercial posture through the only port permitted by the viceroyalty, Los Adaes. Established as the provincial capital in 1721, it was located in the northeast, opposite the French factory of Natchitoces in Louisiana, and remained the capital for almost fifty years, when its powers transferred to San Antonio. In Los Adaes, the two rivals quickly discovered how much easier it was to deal in contraband rather than licit trade.[18]

Contact with the French soon localized between a defensive line paralleling the Mississippi River and the boundaries of the Indian nations inhabiting that area. However, military officials found that the defensive barrier did not limit French-Indian trade. From Fort Orleans, and Forts Cavagnolles in Missouri and Michilimackinac on the Great Lakes, French traders persisted in plying their wares along the frontiers of New Spain. Moving upstream from the tributaries of the Missouri River, they carried on an active commerce with the Plains Indian tribes. In exchange for the horse, which they lacked, the French offered firearms and munitions that presidio captains entrusted only to friendly Indian auxiliaries.[19] Thus, due to shift in international power, plus the serious drain on the royal treasury caused by the support of isolated urban areas, northern Indian rebels once again took on the "outside forces" that were attempting to dominate them. The bitter power struggle came to a head with the reconquest of New Mexico. Governor Diego de Vargas employed the intensified pressure of divide and conquer tactics against the Pueblo Indians. Exploiting existing discord among the Pueblos, he made peace with villages requesting it, promising forgiveness, and at the same time, waged incessant war on those northern pueblos that remained hostile.[20] Using Pueblos to fight Pueblos, Vargas merely implemented a method of warfare advocated by Spaniards since the Chichimeca War. Maestre de Campo José Francisco Marín, who inspected the presidios of Nueva Vizcaya in 1693, stated the policy clearly when he wrote that it would benefit frontier forces to introduce sedition among the Indian nations, "in order that from these greater security for the Spaniards might be born and produced, and in order that, being disunited, they may be suspected and feared by each other; those reduced to the royal obedience may be conserved and maintained through fear of those unreduced."[21] Presidio captains took great care to insure use of this divide and conquer policy against the tribes of the north.

An event that appeared to favor the Pueblos occurred in June of 1696. A number of Pueblo villages revolted again. They killed five missionaries, twenty-one colonists, many soldiers, and burned and desecrated several churches, then fled into the mountains. As a result of the hostility, Governor Vargas mounted a major expedition and suppressed the Pueblo rebels. He persuaded most to return to their pueblos, but others remained in the mountains or fled to Navajo and Hopi country. After this revolt, the Pueblos settled into uneasy relations with the invaders. The governor's methods of pacifying the Pueblos succeeded in bringing Indian leaders into an alliance with the frontier citizenry, but the mutual distrust long prevalent between the two races did not wane nor die even through humanitarian impulses by both Franciscans and the King sought to cement good relations in New Mexico.

In spring of 1705, a year after Governor Vargas died pursuing a band of Faráon Apaches, the fear and futility of fighting off Apache raiders paralyzed New Mexicans. The unsuccessful battles soon depleted the province's resources. The Santa Fe garrison lacked both arms and horses for military reprisals, and the civilian militia was both unwilling and unable to supply the needed manpower for offensives against Faráones, Gileños, and Natagées who ravaged the country. Governor Francisco Cuervo y Valdes, the municipal council at Santa Fe, and the Franciscans appealed jointly to the viceroyalty for military relief. The viceroy and his council met in Mexico City, and noted that, though New Mexico was draining the royal treasury of some 77,500 pesos annually, military supplies and thirty additional troops must be sent to Santa Fe.[22]

Before this relief, when murder and property loss placed New Mexico in constant insecurity, Governor Cuervo somehow managed to raise a campaign force and mount a punitive expedition against Apache warriors who had been stealing horses and cattle from the pueblos of San Ildefonso, Santa Clara, and San Juan. Additionally, the governor deployed squads of soldiers to the various pueblos and pushed frontier settlement southward, founding the Villa de Albuquerque in 1706. By November, his tactics achieved a precarious peace among the Navajos and Apaches. Such peace was temporary since Indian raiders from the Sandia Mountains continued attacks on Río Grande settlements and pueblos whose inhabitants, in turn, mounted punitive expeditions.[23]

In Sonora during these final years of the seventeenth century, religious work expanded under the Society of Jesus. Jesuits founded their first mission congregation among the Seris in 1679, and eight years later Father Eusebio Francisco Kino established a mission district among the Upper Pimas. Following this in 1697, came Spanish expansion and Jesuit penetration into Lower California under Fray Juan María Salvatierra. On the other hand, military officials were reorganizing frontier defenses since Indian sedition had again surfaced in Nueva Vizcaya. Small bands of Indian rebels decimated by smallpox and warfare against northerners were forced into confederacies and retreated into the impregnable Bolsón de Mapimí.[24]

Before the end of the seventeenth century, Spanish residents of Sonora were pleading with the captain-general and governor of Nueva Vizcaya, Juan Isidro Pardiñas Villar de Francos, for militia support and funding to stem the rising tide of Indian resistance. Captain Blas del Castillo, participating in the Sonora Campaigns, informed the governor that the Sumas, Janos, Jocomes, Pimas, and Apaches had allied and were inciting peaceful mission Indians to join in rebellion. The damage being done to his Majesty's subjects was great indeed and Governor Pardiñas implored upon the viceroy to construct new fortifications in the troubled area.[25] Once again, as in the strained mission father/military relationships, conflict of Spanish tactics fostered a flexibility and ingenuity in Indian resistance.

Conscious of the Jesuit presence and their pressures, the King's authorities continued to believe that total war was the only solution to the Indian menace. In Nueva Vizcaya, Maestre de Campo Marín believed the frontier provinces could not be effectively pacified until Indian alliances were effectively eliminated. Yet Viceroys such as the Conde de Galve encouraged the mission order to Hispanicize and reorganize Indian communities. While believing in the futility of this effort, other viceregal officials continued the flow of military regulations to frontier governors, emphasizing, however, that captured rebels be given due process as specified in the Recopilación de leyes de los reynos de las Indias. Specifically, Indian prisoners of war were not to be deported because of the hardships they would suffer in a new environment and because of the serious drain such deportation would place on the royal treasury. But in the early years of the next century, the tactic of deportation, due mostly to the intensity of Indian defiance in Nueva Vizcaya, characterized the Spanish state position.[26]

As a move to reduce military expenses, Royal officials assumed that deportation of Indian hostiles from the northern frontier would bring a definitive peace. In August of 1711, Viceroy Duque de Linares ordered three hundred Indian prisoners of war interned at Parral sent to the viceregal capital in order that they be distributed in repartimiento to the mills and workshops of central Mexico. Once there, royal officials presumed they could be converted, educated, and eventually earn their own living while enjoying the "tranquility" of the central provinces.[27]

Military and political decisions such as deportation only served to increase hit-and-run raiding in the northern provinces, and in the 1700s, Spanish/Indian contacts became a continual round of raids and assaults by Indian hostiles, and punitive military reprisals by presidials or militia units. Indian raiders became increasingly skilled in strategy and techniques of warfare. Frontiersmen in the more outlying communities found themselves at a loss to deal effectively with this threat. Additionally, the increased tax burden required by the war effort caused further bitter resentment from several districts too impoverished to bear the added strain on their budgets.[28] In vain they attempted to battle an Indian people who set their pattern or type of resistance according to the confusions of a larger society. Indian resistance to the Spaniards depended upon given external factors, rebellion, alliance, or acquiescence to the power of a larger geopolitical force.

CHAPTER III

FOOTNOTES

[1]Moorhead, The Presidio, 20. For a more concise look at the revolts, see Elizabeth A.H. John, Storms Brewed in Other Men's Worlds, 98-154.

[2]Numerous studies by France V. Scholes give definitive insights into the church-state struggle in seventeenth century New Mexico. See for example his "Civil Government and Society in New Mexico in the Seventeenth Century," NMHR (January 1935): 71-111; or Troublous Times in New Mexico, 1659-1670.

[3]Jane C. Sánchez, "Spanish-Indian Relations During the Otermín Administration," NMHR 58 (April 1983): 140.

[4]Alonso de Benavides, Fray Alonzo de Benavides' Revised Memorial of 1634, ed. by Frederick Webb Hodge, George P. Hammond, and Agapito Rey, 151.

[5]Forbes, Apache, Navaho, and Spaniard, 150-52.

[6]Charles W. Hackett, ed., The Revolt of the Pueblo Indians of New Mexico and Otermin's Attempted Reconquest, 1680-1682, 1: xxiv-xxviii.

[7]For an interesting interpretation if Indian leadership during the Pueblo Revolt, see Fray Angélico Chávez, "Pohe-Yemo's Representative and the Pueblo Revolt of 1680," NMHR 42 (April 1967):85-126. Other Indian leaders included Nicolás Jonua of San Ildefonso; Domingo Naranjo, a half-Black leader from Santa Clara; Domingo Romero from Tesuque; Cristóbal Yope of San Lazaro; Felipe de Ye from Pecos; and Juan Punssili from Picuris.

[8]Declaration of Juan Lorenzo and Francisco Lorenzo, Río del Norte, December 20, 1681, in Hackett, Revolt of the Pueblo Indians, 2:249-53.

[9]Auto for the conclusion of the opinions of the Junta, La Isleta, January 1, 1882, in Hackett, Revolt of the Pueblo Indians, 2:354-56.

[10]Oakah L. Jones, Jr., Pueblo Warriors and Spanish Conquest, 39-40; Storms Brewed in Other Men's Worlds, 104.

[11]Tomás de Guadalajara, Historia de la tercera rebelión tarahumara, 8, 43-44, 52.

[12]Autos de guerra contra los indios rebeldes de la Real Corona, March 26, 1692, Archivo Hidalgo de Parral, roll 1692.

[13]Testimonio de los autos hechos sobre las providencias dadas en tiempo de don Gabriel de el Castillo Governador de el Parral, 31 de mayo de 1691 hasta 9 de febrero de 1694, Hackett, Historical Documents, 2:290-310.

[14]Auto de don Gabriel del Castillo acerca de la guerra de los Tarahumaras y pimas de Batópilas y la provincia de Sonora, December 1, 1697, Archivo Hidalgo de Parral, roll 1697A.

[15]Respuesta fiscal sobre diferentes puntos de guerra con los indios enemigos del reyno del Parral . . ., April 1, 1698, Hackett, Historical Documents, 2:418-21.

[16]Spicer, Cycles of Conquest, 284.

[17]Castañeda, Our Catholic Heritage in Texas, 2: 33-109, 268-310; Robert S. Weddle, San Juan Bautista: Gateway to Spanish Texas, 47-54.

[18]Bolton, Texas in the Middle Eighteenth Century, 241-50, 340-58, 387-93.

[19]Donald E. Worcester, "The Spread of Spanish Horses in the Southwest," NHMR 20 (January 1945): 1-13.

[20]Forbes, Apache, Navaho, and Spaniard, 237-43, 250-52.

[21]José Francisco Marin to Viceroy Conde de Galve, Parral, September 30, 1693, in Hackett, Historical Documents, 2:403.

[22]Duque de Alburquerque, Junta, Mexico, February 28, 1706, Spanish Archives of New Mexico, State of New Mexico Records Center, at Santa Fe (hereafter cited as SANM), doc. 121.

[23]Fray Juan Alvarez to the Duque de Alburquerque, Santa Fe, April 16, 1706, AGN, PI 36; Francisco Cuervo y Valdés, bando, Santa Fe, March 10, 1705, SANM, doc. 110; Rael de Aguilar certification, Santa Fe, January 10, 1706, in Hackett, Historical Documents, 3:367.

[24]Informe. . .de Sonora. . .que remite a su Magestad el sargento Mayor de Justicia Juan Isidro Pardiñas y Villar de Francos, governador y capitán general de este Reino. 1693, AGI Guadalajara 152; Expediente relativo a la campaña hecho por el governador, Don Manuel San Juan de Santa Cruz contra los indios Cocoyomes, Parral, July 1, 1715, Archivo Hidalgo de Parral, roll 1715 Aa. (hereafter cited as AHP, 1715 Aa).

[25]Pardiñas to Viceroy Conde de Galve, Parral, August 3, 1689, AGN, PI 30.

[26]Marín to Viceroy Conde de Galve, Parral, September 30, 1693, in Hackett, Historical Documents, 2: 355-61, 401, 419.

[27]Proclamation of Viceroy Duque de Linares, Mexico, August 7, 1711, AGI, Guadalajara 164; Autos de Guerra y diligencias practicadas contra los enemigos de la Real Corona, año de 1708, Parral, AHP, 1708b.

[28]Decreto por él que se impone una contribución a los vecinos de Durango para mantener a los indios acolames prisioneros en guerra, año de 1710, Durango, AHP, 1710b.

CHAPTER IV

MISSIONARIES AND BUREAUCRATS:
A CHAOTIC ARRANGEMENT

Indian revolts in northern New Spain relate to the religious mission, and as a characteristic feature of Indian resistance, its strategies and techniques of conversion require examination. As an agency for Hispanic conversion of Indians, the mission contributed dynamically to assimilation of northern tribes. In contrast to missions in central and southern New Spain, those in the north confronted scattered, culturally diverse Indian communities as yet unexploited by other institutions. Correspondingly, beyond it religious function, the northern mission filled some of the same economic roles as the villa, presidio, or mining community. These mission centers drew justification from both religious need and geopolitical expansion, and they opened up the frontier more effectively than any other entity, but in the process, strengthened the Indian conviction that they could fight and defeat secular Spanish authorities.[1]

In northern New Spain, mendicant orders enjoyed notable independence. The Hapsburgs, recognizing the immensity of the imperial task, granted to missionizing orders the rights and prerogatives of parish priests and authority to administer the sacraments. From the viewpoint of secular clergymen, the regulars' privileges represented a disruption of traditional parochial structure, and they hastened to point out the missionaries' abuses. But so long as the Indian mission program held importance, the regulars resisted encroachment and clung to their Church/State efforts. While their activities in central Mexico decreased as the Indian population there declined, their original enthusiasm for the conversion of "heathen souls" endured on the frontier.[2]

In the early colonial period, the evangelical conquest brought many churchmen north, where geographically defined jurisdictions determined the nature of their advance. In western Sonora ran a coastal lowland separated from the rest of New Spain by the towering Sierra Madres, a formidable barrier of dark, forested mountains and deeply etched canyons. The Yaquis, Mayos, Pimas, Tepehuanes, Opatas, and Seris who constructed rancherías in the sierran valleys and surrounding lowlands were assigned to the Society of Jesus for mission settlement. Other Jesuits moved northward along the eastern flank of the Sierra Madre, working among the Tarahumara of Nueva Vizcaya. East of the mountains lay the central plateau, rising high above the coastal plain and sloping gradually to join the grassy plains of Pimería Alta and New Mexico. Here, the Franciscans formulated their mission regulations and legal requirements. Dominicans proselytized along the east coast of Nuevo Santander in a harsher unknown terrain. Mountain ranges there cut them off from their religious associates and barred extensive northward advance, giving them little part in the early settlement of the American Southwest until the late eighteenth century, when they replaced the ejected Jesuits in Lower California.[3]

The Recopilación de las leyes de Indias and the Ordenanzas sobre descubrimientos, which legislated against armed expeditions, placed responsibility for pacification of the frontier chiefly upon missionary orders.[4] Jesuits began this advance coincidentally. Although Franciscans, Augustinians, and Dominicans had pioneered northwest of Mexico, the Society of Jesus received favorable viceregal attention at the crucial time when the Chichimeca War was ending and official Indian policy was being established. Not subscribing to the Royal Patronage, the Society of Jesus had come to central Mexico in 1572, avoided internal friction, and quickly established its position as a vigorous and disciplined missionary order. Viceroy Luis Velasco II, son of a previous and successful viceroy, preferred Jesuits over other regulars, despite their failures in Florida. From the conclusion of the Chichimeca War until their expulsion in 1767, a paz Jesuita helped heighten an Indian sense of autonomy on their northern lands.

While Jesuits advanced into the unexplored northwestern area of Pimería Alta, Franciscans expanded toward the north central plateau. Accompanying Don Juan de Oñate's 1598 expeditions, they opened New Mexico as a promising mission field. Reaching south as far as the upper Conchos River in the 1640s, they then moved downstream toward the Río Grande, establishing Nuestra Señora de Guadalupe (near present day El Paso) in 1659. Their efforts peaked in 1683 when a delegation of Jumano Indians visited El Paso requesting mission aid and troops to protect them from the Nations of the North. Though the insecure Spanish position at El Paso prohibited sending such help into Jumano country, later that year, following another Jumano petition, a small party of Spaniards, mixed-blood soldiery, and Indian allies marched northward to the junction of the Concho and Colorado Rivers in Texas. Since the mission field looked promising, and obviously ready to serve their Order, Franciscans sought a religious establishment in Texas, but their group or "team" approach among the Nations of the North proved unsuccessful. As a basis for bargaining, most Indians contacted would barter for trinkets, clothing, and food, but they refused to accept mission efforts. Specifically, the Caddos strongly rejected the missions and remained unenticed by the material goods that sometimes lured their more southern kinsmen.

To have the tribes renounce war and affirm loyalty to God and King, the "mission" sought to bring Indians into a semblance of community. Broadly speaking, missionaries conceived of religious conversion as a civilizing process and strove for the social and political reorientation of Indian life. Most religious orders energetically founded reducciones (concentrated mission communities) believing them indispensable to Indian pacification.[5] The thrust of their overall plan aimed at salvation of the individual Indian, but it resulted in exploitation by secular society and the eventual widespread loss of lands and waters to Spanish colonists.

Missionaries advocated reducciones to protect Indians from demoralization which might follow from close contact with Spanish colonists and to teach the rudiments of spiritual and temporal society. But the mission was seldom a true reduction, since many tribes remained semi-nomadic throughout the eighteenth century. For a substantial number of Indians who lived and farmed near it in permanent rancherías, the mission did serve as a center, and other scattered families flocked to the church on feast days, managed to visit for confession and gifts, or stayed for a season now and again. Missionaries usually divided into groups of two or three and quickly spread over a frontier, seeking out Indian rancherías. Generally traveling with an interpreter and, if possible, a small Indian escort, they attempted to baptize the Indian leaders of each village, believing other Indians would follow them in conversion as in other matters. If successful, they then expanded their activities by moving into the surrounding countryside establishing administrative units called rectorados, which consisted of several cabeceras and their visitas. Indeed, these were not large mission complexes, but missions interspersed among the mines, haciendas, and towns.[6]

Missionaries first concerned themselves with simple conversion and on the selection of an Indian village as a place of residence. Once a village was designated, a missionary sought the acquisition of land on which to build churches, storehouses, carpentry shops, gristmill, weaving rooms, and homes for those Indians persuaded to settle at the designated cabecera. There they worked to teach husbandry, stock-raising, and various craft industries to make their missions economically sound.[7] The missionaries served as religious instructors, supervisors of cooperative farms, skilled ranchers, and tradesmen. Such versatility attested to their considerable talents, as did the ease with which most of them persuaded Indians to settle at or near their cabeceras. Since their goal was an economically self-sufficient one, they made horticulture the principal mission occupation. But the farming group remained small and still required supplemental economic resources and other foods, and in most missions, a forced compromise allowed Indians to compete in the new economy.[8]

Occasionally the missionaries found aid in the conversion process from Indians who came as settlers, instructors, and models. Tlaxcalans were used in this way in Nueva Vizcaya, Coahuila, and Texas. Tarascans were sent north to Sonora, and Opatas from Sonora relocated and transformed into presidial companies in Pimería Alta. Organizationally, mission settlements imitated the towns in New Spain, with a governor, judge, councilmen, and sheriff, who constituted a deliberative body that assisted the missionary in the maintenance of internal order. The missionaries also appointed church officials as well as Indian officers; however, these captain-protector appointments to Indian office, as they came to be called, were sometimes made arbitrarily and with little inquiry as to tribal status of such individuals.[9]

The religious fathers understood that internal tribal structure disallowed a chieftain to exercise real authority, a peacetime chief to recall war parties, a head chief to speak for all his bands, a whole tribe to make peace or deliver up criminals, or any Indian to regard stealing as a capital offense. The complexities of Indian political and property concepts, the courtesies and involvements of their international law, the superstitions and fears assailing them, and even their methods of warfare did not elude missionaries and occasioned further manipulation. Religious fathers, generally speaking, saw the Indian as socially passive, and proceeded to impose upon him a rigorous daily routine comprised of public devotions, instruction, and religious festivals. A typical day began with morning mass and instruction, followed with several hours of field labor, and ended with evening prayers and instruction, all strictly enforced. The children received an hour's catechetical lesson in the afternoon during which they were divided into groups supervised in songs and recitation by Indian officials. Major feast days caused elaborate spiritual and secular festivities, and tribes gathered from miles around, enlivening the mission with trading, games, and community devotions vis-a-vis the patterns of religious conversion.

Frequently, Indians were taught to play musical instruments. The Jesuits especially believed that the spiritual and temporal wealth of music was an effective means to teach Christian doctrine. They believed Indians had a natural talent for music, song, and dance. Moreover, Indians were fascinated by choirs and bands with stringed instruments and it came to form the core of village pride in many Jesuit missions.[10] One has to be careful, however, not to create a colonial Golden Age of mission harmony.

Life for the mission Indian was far from utopian. Punishment and discipline were used by the missionaries, but it was meted out in a climate of forgiveness and leniency to avoid cause for vengeance. Banishment from the mission community might come for any of the following: doing a hideous thing, setting a bad example, living a scandalous life, being a bad Christian, being drunk or lazy, consistently violating community ordinance, or acting against the common good of the community. It must be understood the Jesuits and Franciscans practiced different complex rules for daily life of the mission, but both shared the apostolic goals of the Catholic Church.

For example, the teaching of Spanish played an important role in the Jesuit program. In the Mexico City area, only a few different languages were spoken, and a missionary mastering one or two could communicate easily. But in the north, where Indians but a few miles apart might speak mutually unintelligible idioms, many missionaries found themselves at a linguistic loss. Language instruction became essential, and the Jesuits required Indian children to memorize the catechism, recite prayers, and listen to daily sermons in Spanish. The doctrina, or catechism, was taught in both languages to assure that Indian children grasped the meaning of the bilingual doctrine.[11] Knowledge of Spanish was diffused not only by means of missionaries. In Nueva Vizcaya, landed estates, farms, and ranches in outlying areas east of the Sierra Madres served mining communities such as San José del Parral-Santa Bárbara and hired Tepehuanes, Tarahumaras, Conchos, and other Indians for seasonal or sometimes year-round work. Thus, many Indian adults acquired a practical spoken Spanish. Sonoran Yaquis, Mayos, Tarahumaras, and Opatas, working the Chihuahua mining district, by association with pobladores and other Spanish residents, quickly learned the conquerors' language; others, segregated in barrios as at Parral, also received access to the spoken language.[12]

But in more distant areas, such a New Mexico, less culture contact between Indians and frontiersmen complicated language transferral. There, the diverse population of the informal mining towns drew fewer racial distinctions. Further, Franciscan missionaries had an easier time keeping the tightly-knit Pueblos away from Spanish influence. Some Indians labored on ranches, toiled as household servants, and others, impressed through contract labor, worked on various governors' projects. But until workable relations developed between Pueblos and Spaniards after suppression of the Pueblo Revolt, diffusion of Spanish as a means of communication remained insignificant. Moreover, even though culture contact appeared to be greater in Sonoran mining towns, haciendas, and ranches, adults often studied Christian teachings in their native language.[13]   Referring to the Eudebes and Opatas, Jesuit Father Ignaz Pfefferkorn wrote that frequent contact with frontier people and the knowledge of Spanish "thus gained, the customary barter of mutual necessities, but most important the teaching of Christian charity inculcated in them by the missionaries, all of these gradually dispelled their ill feeling and made them friendly toward the Spaniards." [14]

For northern New Spain then, the mission fathers developed a set of rules and precepts that concentrated on doctrinal education and on economic reorganization. Furthermore, the permanence and stability they provided to northern Indian people created a new sense of political and cultural unity among many ranchería communities.[15] Indians responded to the missions, interpreting the new teaching as doctrine compatible with their own, and allowing both to exist simultaneously. Moreover, each tribal group or band possessed its own complex of religious ceremonies and beliefs, and certain components--animism, earth-mother/corn-goddess cults--were compartmentalized into a new doctrine. Observing achievements of medicine men, or hechiceros, many fathers proclaimed them witchcraft to be rooted out and destroyed. Indian rites similar to Christian ritual posed special problems for some religious fathers. Creator myths and cult heroes implied Indian knowledge of the existence of God, and confession of sins corresponded to like Christian duties.   Some missionaries rejected such coincidences of faiths as ingenious works of medicine men, mockers and parodies of the true religion.[16]

In the case of Sonoran Indians, father Juan Nentvig commented that the nature of the Indian world view was so variable that it was just too hard to explain. His opinion, in thirteen years of dealing with Indians, was that their nature revolved on four traits: ignorance, ingratitude, inconstancy, and laziness. Their lives, he believed, focused upon these peculiarities.[17] But the actions of individual leaders, especially those recently admitted into the church, particularly disturbed Father Nentvig, "a single malcontent or one puffed-up egotist with a sorcerer's reputation such as Luis de Sáric is enough to stir up an entire nation."[18]

On the frontier, potential mission Indians were neither sedentary nor docile, and the intense Indian resistance forced some missionaries and Spanish settlers to unite. But because life in northern New Spain involved not only common defense, but also divisive competition for economic resources, the alliance was a brittle one. The smoldering conflict between clergy and Spanish ranchers, miners, or merchants over Indian lands and labor remained constant, welling up time and again in bitter, mutually destructive bloodshed.[19] Extremely poor relations existed in areas with well-established rectorados and expanding neighboring mixed-blood communities. Secularization of missions, based on the ten-year law whereby a secular priest replaced the regular, thus releasing coveted lands and labor, brought intense pressure on a mission father who for one reason or another refused to relinquish his vested interest in the Indians. But as long as his mission served to protect frontier Indian communities, as long as the king encouraged no one else to do this job, the missionary continued presiding over and defending his Indian converts. Furthermore, mission fathers made it very difficult for Spanish miners, merchants, and hacendados to compete for Indian land and Indian labor.[20]

A case in point is the Tarahumara country, two hundred miles in width--from the 106th meridian to the 109th--and in some areas as much as two hundred forty miles in length--from the 26th to the 30th parallels. Scattered over approximately five thousand square miles of territory, Tarahumara people were bordered on the southeast by the Tepehuán, on the east and north by the Concho and Toboso, on the northwest by the Jova, Opata and lower Pima and on the west by the Guazapar and the Guarohío. That these Indians were neighbors did not mean that their environments in Nueva Vizcaya were identical. They lived under a variety of different conditions and resisted the conquest of their homeland in a variety of different ways.

The basic settlement pattern of the Tarahumara allowed for greater armed resistance to the colonizers. The ranchería was an established community which permitted a half-sedentary, half-nomadic existence. In the summer and fall, the Tarahumara concentrated their rancherías around well-watered and favored hillside spots. In the winter, they moved the households to the sheltered arroyos of the valley floors. Ranchería farming was the major family activity, and families, aided by isolation and the lack of any great Jesuit or Franciscan penetration in their area, used the ranchería as a source of resistance to hacendados, merchants, and miners.

Throughout the seventeenth century, from Santa Bárbara and Chihuahua, from the Tarahumara homelands of Yepómera and San Pablo, Spanish residents labored to sustain and defend their frontier settlements while extracting what rewards they could from the Tarahumara Indians and the province's richly veined sierras. But land grants were made to influential northern families, the more affluent of which founded few landed estates. In most cases, the mestizo colonists, or vecino, expected to defend his own lands and go to the rescue of others at the king's request, was a more common sight. The prosperous areas of occupation were the lands taken from Tarahumara Indians south of the Río Conchos and the immediate areas surrounding San José del Parral. Both Jesuits and the small Spanish population favored this particular region because the best agricultural lands were situated there, as were the larger concentration of Indians.

Highland Indian communities, on the other hand, were given rights to land as local territorial groups, not as kinship units. Political power was placed in the hands of Indian officials, usually assigned visiting Jesuit missionaries, and the rapid growth of missions after the 1630s gave to Tarahumara parishioners a new series of organized and stable associations through which a new personal and communal identification might readily be expressed. Thus, the king's bureaucrats in New Spain's far northern frontier attempted to concentrate the Indian population but also to shift traditional land tenure to the favor of Spain.

By mid-century, Spanish colonists had penetrated the rugged geography of highland Tarahumara country and proceeded as in the past, to organize labor for mining, agriculture and ranching. The Indians, however, did not command the economically developed skills and resources to participate in the development of grand enterprises for profit. In Tarahumara country the Indians were not forced to supply labor to the new mining/agricultural enterprises, nor were they barred from direct participation in the returns. The Indians were not transformed into ordinary subjects fattening the king's coffers. Rather, a mestizo laborer developed, who continued to draw greater share of his subsistence from his own efforts on his ranchland, or labor in the local mines and haciendas.

From the Spanish entrepreneur's point of view, Indians remained under paternalistic Jesuit control which could maintain itself at no cost to his self-interest, especially the silver mines of the San José del Parral district. This served to maintain the importance of land in Tarahumara life. At the same time, land in the hands of the Indians had to be limited in amount, or they would not have possessed sufficient incentive to offer potential labor after secularization. In this regard Visitor General Juan de Cervantes Casaus, reporting to the viceroy in the 1650s, devised a plan for pueblos of pardoned Indians who would be continually monitored by Indian officials.[21]   Although the plan was not carried out, changes in general conditions of the ranchería communities did assure frontiersmen a sufficient seasonal supplement to their small number of resident mestizo laborers. This was accomplished through the "mission of the Tarahumara," or the mission province as co-extensive with the political province. By restricting the amount of land in the hands of each Indian community to an area of six and one-half square miles, the frontier economy grabbed sufficient lands and water for mining/ranching activities.[22]

Indian residents in the mission reducciones were distributed in labor-drafts to the leading Indian officials, who by law, were permitted to oblige 4 percent of the mission Indians to work for them, provided they observed the regulations regarding the going wage of half a real per day, the provision of food during travel to place of work, and humane working conditions. Regardless of the regulations, the 4 percent quota was regularly exceeded and some forced impressment by Indian officials themselves continued through the seventeenth century. Interesting enough, by 1650, the majority of mine laborers in the mining camps of the San José del Parral district were not Tarahumara, but mestizos and castas who formed their own barrios of fundidores, barreteros and tenateros, or working class laborers.

In order to take better advantage of the colonial economic system, evade taxes and other governmental regulations frontier people tried to locate their haciendas or mines close to exploitable labor pools. Yet the scattering of settlements was, in part, an outgrowth of the province's particular mining/agricultural requirements. In a region where fertile land was scarce, mestizo households were scattered along stream valleys. Despite defense considerations, they continued to move into the more distant frontier. A few critics of this dispersed pattern of living claimed that the mestizo settler-stockman intransigence was the principal barrier to the organization and management of charted Indian communities.[23]

Whatever may have been the concern of the particular groups involved, the king's more ordinary subjects paid lip service to a program for Indian incorporation which was guided by mission reorganization of Indian communities. They themselves were guided by economic self-interest and a sharp sense of survival. In theory, the basic ideal of what the missionaries wanted to accomplish among the Indians was defined as religious conversion. When that program was repeatedly interrupted by slave-raiding, kingly meddling or other illegal forays, the resulting conflicts was generally resolved in favor of the king's laws and the mission fathers. The ultimate goal pursued by the determined and assertive Jesuit and Franciscan Orders was the conversion of Indians and their gradual economic incorporation into frontier Spanish society.

To Spanish colonizers, most as adventurer settler-stockman types, the bloodshed of the Chichimeca Wars, the disturbing autonomy which the king of Spain seemed to allow the mission evangelist was not to be encouraged. Many crown representatives, official and unofficial, were openly hostile to the social integration of Indian nations. It is not difficult to understand why, even before Indian resistance, the Jesuits or Franciscans had difficulty in implementing their mission programs. If there had been no suspicion of them, particularly from local governors and more ordinary Spanish residents, they possibly might have fared better.

Throughout the seventeenth century, front-line missionary persuaders of kingly authority, socially and economically reorganized distinct linguistic/cultural Indian communities into productive mission centers. This consolidation was pressed home with great vigor throughout the North, and in the Tarahumara region it had a profound impact. That is, mission reduction occurred; a uniformity of plans prevailed. But by mid-century, the Audience de Guadalajara was complaining that management and civilizing efforts had failed among this particular group of Indian people.[24] The Tarahumara people supposedly remained far more dispersed than other northern tribes, and it was this wide scattering, with no pattern for urban living, that blocked the overall master plan of socializing Indians. Failure, of course, they also attributed to the intrusion of the missionaries. With few exceptions, it was believed that the missions were genuine centers of Indian resistance. From the beginning, the Jesuits introduced a new ceremonial center into Indian society that served as an element of wider social integration in the Indian lifeway.[25]

For reasons connected with the general weakness of the Hapsburg Crown, the "mission of the Tarahumara" turned out to be very different from that which had been planned. In Nueva Vizcaya, the movement began unevenly and was weakly supported by an impoverished royal government. It was not until the 1630s that the Order organized and began its first permanent mission among the Tarahumara; in spite of natural barriers, it began to make strides northward. During the next thirty-years, the Jesuits were in the forefront of frontier advance, founding mission cabeceras in the heart of the Tarahumara homeland. Yet, except for the Santa Bárbara-Parral environs, where the Order received special military support because of the many scattered mining camps and towns, the general mission movement was not only assuming responsibility for Tarahumara spiritual needs, but also their social, political, and economic needs.[26] By 1648, a large number of adults, as well as their children, were baptized in the sacred faith, memorized its prayers and mysteries and received the water of Holy Baptism. They were gathered into towns, whereas previously they had been scattered in several rancherías. Three missionaries worked among them; and after the Indians were somewhat pacified, churches were built and dedicated. The common enemy, however, could hardly bear to see so many souls escape from its claws, for the remainder of the Indians who lived in the mountains far removed from the missions asked for priests to come and work among them. Mission fathers responded to this call and prepared to go into the interior to gather, instruct and baptize the inhabitants who lived along the more northern edges of the Tarahumara frontier.[27]

At these mission stations, missionaries, such as Father Geronimo de Figueroa, began to expand their efforts. From the frontier mission of San Felipe, he worked his way northward, across the Río Conchos, and was later joined by the Jesuits José Pascual, Gabriel Díaz and Cornelio Godinez. Despite hostilities from some Indian chieftains, who threatened to kill them, the Jesuits, under the proctorship of Indian captains, had settled some of the widely scattered Tarahumara rancherías. But, for the most part, they were greatly overextended.

Aside from obtaining obedience to His Majesty, an important task of the Jesuits was that of making their mission economically self-sufficient. Because Father Godinez' Indian converts were becoming restless, fields had to be brought into production and immediately so that food could support the mission population and provide an economic surplus to hold newly converted Tarahumaras. Gift-giving helped induce some Indians to stay until the fields were harvested. Later, free from tribute payments, individual lots were assigned to resettled families, with Father Godinez supervising their care and instructing his Indian subjects in agricultural methods, homemaking, land management, and Christianity.[28] By now more Tarahumara headmen acquired skills and were gradually organized into an Indian governorship that answered to both Indian and Jesuit alike. Some became missionary specialists encouraging, supervising, and assisting in the instruction of religious doctrine. Others, became militia captains, ready at any moment to respond to military action.

With respect to gobernadores (popularly elected Indian officials), the Society of Jesus had great success. After two years work, Luis de Valdes y Rejano, the new governor of Nueva Vizcaya, formally appointed Indian gobernadore captains of San Gerónimo, Huejotitlán, and of other nearby pueblos.[29] Missionary progress continued; by 1648, nine years after beginning, about five thousand Tarahumara had been resettled into six mission cabeceras and their visitas. But, from Father Pascual's perspective, this was an unhealthy growth, for it depended less on voluntary consent than on the threat of peace by persuasion.[30] Although he does not mention this, it can be deduced from the geographical pattern of the missions--some were situated on the edges of the northwestern frontier, and others were placed near chartered towns--the Jesuits were thus advancing and consolidating the frontier, establishing Jesuit hegemony beyond the Conchos into enemy territory, and moving friendly Tarahumara behind this imaginary line.

This pattern of concurrent advance and retreat of the missions corresponded with advance of the mining frontier. In northern Nueva Vizcaya or what the Jesuits called Alta Tarahumara, the Jesuits had to choose between living among their converts on the frontier, thereby risking either martyrdom or the loss of their converts, or relocating them close to San José del Parral or Durango. Among these older established rectorados (administrative units) the Indians could neither rebel nor run away, but they were also susceptible to corruption by castas or mestizos. This was perhaps a radical missionary change in the highlands of Nueva Vizcaya. A general migration by renegade Indians was toward the west and south.

Gerónimo de Figueroa responded to this threat by establishing San Felipe de Jesús near the Indian strongholds. But the majority of missions south of the Río Conchos were Indian governed communities, a program designed to prevent potential bloodshed. Obviously, the uses of a dual missionary policy introduced a balance in priest-Indian relations--helping to hide the benign absolutism of the Jesuit system. The history of the Tarahumara mission by mid-century, therefore, illustrated the success of a geopolitical policy on the missionary frontier. In fact, the Tarahumara accepted more aspects of the mission program than they rejected. But they refused to discontinue a number of their prehispanic customs including their seasonal drinking festival, or tesgüinada. But even there the Jesuits met with some success. In the village of San Felipe, according to Padre José Pascual,

> Drunkenness, which is unquestionably the most prevalent vice in this nation, has been controlled in this village. If the Indians do congregate to drink, they do it in an out-of-way place so as not to be seen. Everyone participates in this debauchery--young and old, men and women. The old ones start the dances. The lectures given them on the evils of drunkenness are responsible for the control of this vice.[31]

Introduction of the Jesuit mission program immediately inserted in Indian society the issue of acceptance of an order prescribed for them. While acceptance of the spiritual dimension occurred in Tarahumara, a strong contingent of Indians remained outside its influence. After the rebellion of 1648, the Jesuits classified this region north of the Río Conchos as unbaptized, or pagan. Instead, those northern communities which military officials had labeled as "savages" appeared as an important element within Indian society. These communities fought the assimilative tendencies of colonial society and, despite strong repressive measures, they continued to shift settlement patterns in avoidance of missions, towns or mines. They were the communities continually labeled as harboring Indian hechiceros.

In Indian country, as indicated earlier, the king's frontline officials recognized and granted immunities to a handpicked Indian leadership, but this was done more in defiance of the development of a renegade Indian leadership. Hence, concurrent with the renegade movement in the highlands of Nueva Vizcaya, throughout the countryside and during the entire seventeenth century, persons of this class were known as Indian captains. This elite was granted special labor exemptions and a number of legal privileges, such as permission to ride horses, to dress like Spaniards, to carry swords and to call themselves "señor." Men such as the Indian leader Don Pablo were occasionally granted royal coats of arms and other insignia. Some Indian men owned large herds of sheep and cattle. Those believed most trustworthy were given the responsibility of governing entire districts, known officially as the captain-protector system, and nearly all seem to have held municipal offices, the result being the creation of a modified local government staffed by Indian officials.[32]

Apache Warrior

In practice, by introducing the captain-protector system into the "mission of the Tarahumara," the king's officials fostered a politically sophisticated Indian leadership that served to intercede between developing Spanish society on the one hand and the intransigent Jesuit society on the other. Captain-protectorships, regarded as a sign of honor and prestige, were limited in each gathered community to a relatively small group, the members of which served repeatedly as gobernadores (elected officials) for both Spanish bureaucrats and mission fathers.

After almost forty years of Spanish sponsorship, the program had divided ranchería communities into three factions: the mission sites, whose gobernadores favored the Jesuits, the border rancherías of the highland frontier, whose people split over acceptance or rejection of colonial society; and those isolated sierra hideaways whose Indian leaders were either men who had never tasted mission life or who were vigorous, anti-Spanish rebels. Except or a few minor variations, this arrangement would be the real source of Spanish insecurity. The nature of the problem is best appreciated by observing the movement into the northeastern half of Tarahuara country.

The late missionary movement, not actually advancing in northeastern Tarahumara country until 1678, promised to be more successful than the one from 1639 to 1678--a period coinciding with some procrastination in the frontier government. Unlike the earlier movement, which had risen spontaneously and had been rather strongly supported locally, the subsequent one was guaranteed some military and financial support. Still, the movement was carried out almost single-handedly by Jesuits such as Tomás de Guadalajara, who opted for living among frontier Indian people rather than removal of the Indians into gathered cabeceras. Indeed, it was this policy change that made the highland frontier seem less promising than it had at the outset.[33]

This change of emphasis in the overall administrative program increased Indian resistance to an encompassing frontier society. In the highlands of Tarahumara country, while some rancherías were infiltrated by the Jesuits, many were not. This made it difficult to displace traditional society. What military officials least appreciated was that certain Indian renegades, allied with the Conchos living near the frontier, had the active support of the more established mission cabeceras south of Concho territory. Thus in 1673, Governor José García de Salcedo at Parral initiated the resettling of suspected rebels into missions near the chartered towns. In addition, and apparently with the support of Indian Captain Don Marcos, Captain Francisco de Elizondo relocated a group of Tarahumara indios amigos near the presidio of San Francisco de Conchos.[34]

The basis of the mission program in northeastern Tarahumara, successful in the earlier mission movement, was in the building of a sense of community among rancherías. The approach was cautious, seeking to create a loose federation of dispersed rancherías to a central force of mission community. This sense of Indian community, separate from secular society, was to foster serious contentions between the mission fathers and the new, struggling Spanish communities. A sharply defined political conflict between Spanish society and the Jesuit mission system continually undermined Indian welfare.[35]

It is obvious that the twin themes which dominated the frontier, protection of Indian people and economic development of the north, were governed by expansion of the mines. So many miners had been killed that mining was a precarious business. But at San José del Parral, Cerro de Mercado, Santa Bárbara, Cuencamé, Indé, and other camps, volunteer wage earners outnumbered drafted workers by ten to one. The mines relied upon free labor, supplemented by an assortment of slaves, some Indian, but mainly Blacks, suitable for work in the refining mills. The labor force in these mines with their transient population of mestizo miners, traders, Spanish officials and a labor force of free Indian migrants from the south was supplemented by a small number of part-time Indian laborers. Consequently, in mining communities where production was modest, forced labor was not a result.[36]

Tarahumara rebels, effectively isolated themselves from the struggling Spanish economy. For the majority, wage labor assumed another facet. Rather than being a routine feature of Indian life, Indian people resorted to it only occasionally. In their mission centers they maintained a separate economy which consisted of subsistence agriculture and stock raising, supplemented by small amounts of clandestine trade with the far northern tribes. Among these isolated missions, the sense of community remained strong. But because of the recurrent disruption of community life resulting from Spanish pressure for Indian labor, individuals were frequently forced to work outside of their mission areas. This resulted in the wasting of their fields or breakup of their isolated rancherías by militia/presidio punitive campaigns. It must be understood that this affected the people in a uneven way. The Indian leadership was unable, moreover to maintain solidarity in the face of relocation into mission communities. In a sense, missions in Tarahumara country inspired a sense of common destiny. The Indians seemed trapped between two dissimilar cultures and, therefore, reacted against Spanish bureaucracy and its demands in a nonmilitary fashion. These reactions took the form of religious movements that often arose after the suppression of bloody revolts. They reinforced Indian solidarity through a supposed new faith in hechicero leadership. It must be stressed, though, that these movements represented culminations in the feelings of hostility and in the exaltation of the Tarahumara's past life. They were nativistic in that the movements defined and gave meaning to a separate form of resistance and pride in Indian heroes.

Indians of the highland areas, then, came to grips with Spain's Indian policy. They maintained the status of autonomous communities, providing their own subsistence on scarce land, and tended to continue this arrangement throughout this indecisive frontier period. The actual threat to Tarahumara livelihood and culture, however, came not only from the mixture of Spanish humanitarianism and punitive military campaigns, but also from community pressures. Natural population increase within their sierra hideouts decreased the amount of land available to community members, as did an unrestricted migration from other missions. Thus, as long as possible, Indian leaders tended to push off surplus population into newly formed Jesuit visitas of the north.[37] More importantly, the Tarahumara leadership in the high sierras strove to force community members to redistribute any pool of accumulated wealth which could potentially be used to alter land tenure in favor of a few ranchería families. The purchase of goods in the villas or pueblos also ranked as a major social threat and was discouraged, for it displayed a willingness to share in useful baggage (food, clothing, and firearms) of the mestizo or casta vecinos. They also refused to discontinue a number of their other prehispanic customs including the seasonal ceremonies, which further bound the Indians together and provided escape from the hardships of their struggle. Overall, the Tarahumara did not fail to capitalize on the bitter conflict between the Jesuits and secular society, and their grievances continued to be land encroachment, and exploitation by the small Spanish population in the region.[38]

Indeed, the Tarahumara ensured their survival by accepting wage labor opportunities, which was greatly stimulated by the "pull" of the mines. At the same time that they actively participated in the struggling Spanish economy, they retained control of their mission communities, which remained tribute free. They seemed to well-understand the balance of power tactics they employed, and when all else failed--they rebelled.

CHAPTER IV

FOOTNOTES

1Herbert E. Bolton, "The Mission as a Frontier Institution in the Spanish-American Colonies," American Historical Review 23 (October 1917): 46-47.

2Robert Ricard, The Spiritual Conquest of Mexico: An Essay on the Apostolate and the Evangelizing Methods of the Mendicant Orders in New Spain: 1532-1572, trans. by Lesley Byrd Simpson, 5-7, 15-38.

3John Kessell, Friars, Soldiers, and Reformers, Hispanic Arizona and the Sonora Mission Frontier, 1767-1856, 13-25.

4In 1573, Felipe II banned the term conquest in the New World, preferring instead the term pacification of the frontier. See for example, Lewis Hanke, The Spanish Struggle for Justice in the Conquest of America, 130-31.

5Charles W. Polzer, Rules and Precepts of the Jesuit Missions of Northwestern New Spain, 5-10.

6Ibid.

7Richard Schutz, "Jesuit Missionary Methods in Northwestern Mexico, "Journal of the West 8 (January 1969): 76-89.

8Theodore E. Treutlein, "The Economic Regime of the Jesuits in Eighteenth-Century Sonora," Pacific Historical Review 8 (September 1939): 289-300.

9For a description of how political incorporation worked in practice see Theodore E. Treutlein, ed. Ignaz Pfefferkorn: Sonora, A Description of the Province, 266-83.

10Theodore E. Treutlein, ed., Missionary in Sonora, The Travel Reports of Joseph Och, S.J., 1755-1767, 120; Polzer, Rules and Precepts, 46-47.

11Polzer, Rules and Precepts, 51.

12Spicer, Cycles of Conquest, 425.

13Polzer, Rules and Precepts, 51.

14Treutlein, Pfefferkorn, 243-44.

15Polzer, Rules and Precepts, 5-12.

16Spicer, Cycles of Conquest, 297.

17Juan Nentvig, S.J., Rudo Ensayo, A Description of Sonora and Arizona in 1764 (Ed. by Alberto Francisco Pradeu and Robert R. Rasmussen), 55.

66   INDIAN REVOLTS IN NORTHERN NEW SPAIN

[18]Ibid.

[19]Richard, The Spiritual Conquest of Mexico, 285-86.

[20]María Teresa Huerta, Rebeliones indígenas en el Noreste de Mexico, 13.

[21]1Informe de Juan de Cervantes Casaus al virrey, fechado en San José del Parral, October 1, 1654, AGN, Presidios II.

[22]Robert C. West, The Mining Community in Northern New Spain, 49-55.

[23]Governor José García de Salcedo to the king, Parral, March 4, 1674, AGI, Guadalajara 145.

[24]Audiencia de Guadalajara to the King, Guadalajara, March 3, 1653, AGI, 143.

[25]Schmutz, "Jesuit Missionary Methods in Northwestern Mexico," 76.

[26]Autos sobre si convendría la elección de obispados en el Nuevo Mexico y doctrinas de Sinaloa, 1639, folio 13, AGI, Guadalajara 138.

[27]Noticias de la misiones sacadas de la anua del Padre José Pascual; ano de 1651, Documentos-Mexico, 3:179.

[28]Ibid.

[29]Noticias de José Pascual, San Felipe, June 29, 1652, Documentos-Mexico, 3:209.

[30]Ibid.

[31]Noticias de José Pascual, San Felipe, June 29, 1652, Documentos-Mexico, 3:209.

[32]Francisco Alegre, Historia de la compañía, 2:463-65.

[33]José Tarda and Tomás de Guadalajara to Provincial, Francisco Xímenes, February 2, 1676, Documentos-Mexico, 3:279-82.

[34]Autos de las campañas de García de Salcedo se inician en Cuencamé, AGI, Guadalajara 145.

[35]Alegre, Historia de la compañía, 2: 463-65.

[36]West, The Mining Community in Northern New Spain, 49-55; María Teresa Huerta, Rebeliones indígenas, 60-62.

[37]Tomás de Guadalajara, Historia de la tercera rebelión tarahumara, ed. by Roberto Ramos, 30-40.

[38]María Elena Galaviz, Rebeliones indígenas en el Norte de la Nueva España, 73-78.

CHAPTER V

FRONTIER WARFARE: A
LEGACY OF REVOLT, 1724-1754

Neglected by the Hapsburgs, New Spain's northern frontier maintained a great degree of local autonomy that preempted any officially directed attitude or action. Spain's royal officials and local presidio captains dealt independently with Indian hostilities since from viceroy to presidio commander, frontier authority hung from a loose chair of command. In part, the unprecedented dimensions of the presidial task, the inadequacy of manpower and other resources allocated to it, the unclear division or responsibility between provincial governors and presidio captains, worked to the advantage of Indian rebels. Further weakening of the provincial governing structure came from a missionary program that consciously or unconsciously, pitted local governors, hacendados, and presidio commanders against one another.

But in order to revitalize New Spain and create new sources of revenue, the Bourbon monarchy encouraged economic development of the north. Some fifty years prior to Charles III himself, Brigadier Pedro de Rivera investigated conditions on the northern frontier. Accompanied by a military engineer, two assistants, and five scribes, Brigadier Rivera spent three and a half years completing an extensive three thousand-league visit to twenty-two scattered presidios. Issued in late 1728, Rivera's report recommended reduction of frontier presidios and cuts in soldiers' salaries,[1] and it led to the viceroy's famous Reglamento of 1729, designed to place Indian policy under a reorganized military authority. Specifics of the Reglamento prohibited attacks on hostile tribes unless efforts to achieve peace by persuasion failed, banned royal officials from siding with one tribe against another unless one of them specifically requested such assistance, and ordered presidio soldiers to refrain from creating unrest among Indians and exploiting them economically. And, whenever Indian renegades sued for peace, presidio captains were to accept, but only after a written and signed agreement by the Indians to accept Christianity and the king's rule.[2]

Overall, the changes were revolutionary, and until 1810, Spanish officials presided over virtually autonomous domains. An immediate measure taken by Viceroy Casafuerte obtained some results. In an attempt to solve the renegade problem in Coahuila and Nueva Vizcaya, using much the same method successful in the Chichimeca War of the late 1500s, Casafuerte in 1723 extended the olive branch to the Acoclames, Cocoyomes, Chisos, and other Indian nations. He centralized the previously mismanaged payment of peace tribute, prohibited inhumane treatment of prisoners of war, and sought an alliance with the Tepehuán and Tarahumara Indians to end their hit-and-run tactics in Nueva Vizcaya. But as warfare increased in intensity and spread to nearby mining centers, the viceroy felt impelled to recommend forced Indian relocation to the Caribbean presidios of

Havana, Santa Domingo, and Puerto Rico. In May, more than three hundred men, women, and children were captured and marched to Vera Cruz under "heavy guard and collars" for shipment aboard the Armada of Barvolento. According to Juan Francisco Mendoza, 138 Indians simply sickened and died on the march, while another 83 managed to escape near the mountains of Vera Cruz.[3] The rest eventually were shipped to the Caribbean. Casafuerte succeeded in temporarily quitting Indian attacks from out of the inaccessible Bolsón de Mapimí.

Within the vast area of the Chihuahua desert, Coahuila, and southwestern Texas, various pressured Apache bands moved southward, and in Nueva Vizcaya, Tarahumara rebels joined Gileños of the north to raid settlements north of Chuihuahua. From the banks of the Conchos River, ranchería Tobosos and Conchos, their numbers depleted by warfare and disease, assimilated with nomadic Apache bands, thereby augmenting the Apache threat to the frontier. Natagées, Mescaleros, and Lipánes also constructed their rancherías in this area on the northern side of the Río Grande. The Natagées settled near El Paso and regularly criss-crossed the border, north to join Gila Apaches in southern New Mexico and south to raid northern Nueva Vizcaya and El Paso itself. Southeast of them the Mescaleros moved in, establishing rancherías in the mountains of southwestern Texas. On their raids, they crossed the Río Grande to attach Chihuahua in the west and from their refuge in the Bolsón de Mapimí, they harassed haciendas and towns as far west as Saltillo.[4] Along the lower reaches of the Río Grande lived the Lipánes. These people moved onto the plains and into the mountain on both sides of the Río Grande, and sometimes joined Mescaleros on punishing raids into Nueva Vizcaya. Primarily confining their strikes to eastern Coahuila in the neighborhood of Monterrey, they occasionally turned north to plunder in Texas among missions and Spanish communities near the presidio of San Antonio de Béjar.[5]

The Nations of the North and the Comanches ranged within Texas. From the early 1700s on, Comanches, emerging from the Rocky mountains, swept across the Texas plains, driving Apaches before them and raiding New Mexico and Texas settlements. Three major tribal divisions characterized the Comanches: Yupes (people of the Timber) and Yamparicas (Root-eaters), who ranged northward form the Arkansas River, and Cuchanecs (Buffalo-eaters), who roamed southward form the Arkansas deep into Texas, Coahuila, Nueva Vizcaya, and New Mexico. The Cuchanecs' (also called Orientales) major subdivision, the Ietan, eventually came to terms with the Wichitas and their French allies in Texas. During the 1760s Comanches crossed the Río Grande to attack Lipán rancherías as well as isolated settlements.[6]

Neighboring New Mexico's situation differed little from the rest of the northern frontier. Apaches roamed in the mesas and wide stretches of desert and dry arroyos in the central part of the province. Navajos in the northwest also ranged into New Mexico and, allied with Gileño kinsmen from the south, raided Sonora and Nueva Vizcaya. North of the Navajo lived the Utes, coming from mountain retreats to foray into the province. East of the Río Grande, various bands of Faráon Apaches, Jicarillas, Sandias, and Organos, in alliance with Natagées, swept in and out of New Mexico freely. Near the Mogollón Mountains to the south, other Apache bands ambushed caravans traveling along the river and struck settlements in Nueva Vizcaya and Sonora. The king's more ordinary vassals, mestizos and castas for the most part, moving into Indian territory, fought never ending battles with these frontier warriors.[7]

By 1730, the powerful Comanches, allied with Utes, had driven the Apaches from their northern ranges and enjoyed unimpeded access to the province. As the Apaches before them, they brought stock, plunder, and captives to trade markets at eastern pueblos. Such methods of trading generated tension. New Mexican pobladores and Pueblo Indians tended to exploit their eastern customers while Comanches often abused New Mexican hospitality by stealing cattle and horses, thereby terrorizing the province. High prices, fees for trading privileges at pueblos, restrictions on the sale of such items as guns and horses, and rudeness to outsiders invited Comanche hostility. Indian raids and exemplary reprisals increased chances of violent encounter. Yet New Mexico desperately needed the commerce, and despite the danger provincial officials encouraged Comanche trade. Indeed, Taos Pueblo soon developed into the major trading center of the far north.

In September of 1725, New Mexico's governor attempted to minimize friction by supervising the trade. Governor Juan Domingo de Bustamante instructed local alcaldes to oversee the trading to prevent any disturbances of the peace. He also warned them to respect the rights of the two parties to barter freely.[8] When problems continued, the determined governor tried more elaborate regulations to defend the "royal jurisdiction," and in the summer of 1726, prosecuted seven New Mexicans for taking advantage of Indians seeking to trade slaves and furs at Pecos. Royal officials even established specific hours for traders to barter with Indians, but such economic stipulations fell far short of curbing dishonest trading practices of both governmental and private participants.

In 1737, the new governor, Enrique de Olvide y Michelina, issued another ruling prohibiting anyone from trading with Indians or visiting their camps without royal license, be he Pueblo or Spaniard.[9] This edict not only failed to establish ethical trading practices, but its regulation of visits to Indian encampments caused increased Indian hostility. Also, a falling out between the Comanches and Utes prompted fifty years of warfare between the two and exacerbated problems in New Spain's northernmost frontier. Utes settled their differences with the Pueblos, Jicarillas, and other Apache nations, and presented the colonial government with a strong front against Indian hostile. But Comanches resented the idea of an alliance with their former friends and, to retaliate, they stepped up their ambushes in eastern New Mexico, forcing abandonment of many ranches, farms, and Pueblo villages.[10]

To disarm this explosive resentment, New Mexicans mounted ruthless retaliatory expeditions. Rather than punitive offensive campaigns, these raids equalled those they themselves suffered. The frontiersmen sought stock, plunder, and captives saleable as slaves for civilian households. Once they sighted a Comanche camp, their method of combat rivaled in barbarity with that of the Indians. On March 21, 1741, Governor Gaspar de Mendoza, reminded by missionaries of royal policy toward Indians, acted to halt the bloodshed. He banned mistreatment of defenseless women and children and ordered that prisoners of war be treated humanely. Governor Joaquín Codallos y Rabal issued an even stiffer ordinance three years later, re-alerting His Majesty's subjects to their responsibility of peaceful persuasion and Christian conversion of the Indians.

Offenders caught violating his ordinance would be punished severely, with soldiers suffering the harshest penalties--even death if necessary.[11]

A war of nerves developed between the Comanches and New Mexicans. Comanches continued both trading at Taos and terrorizing the pueblos of Pecos and Galisteo. In a few years, they killed 150 Pecos Indians. Finding that neither trade regulations nor restraint in retaliation curbed the attacks, Governor Codallos sought to prohibit Comanche trade altogether. He also suspected Taos Indians of informing Comanches of roving patrols in the area, and in an effort to halt the practice, restricted the Taoseños to within three miles of their pueblo. Both attempts failed, and Comanches participated in the Taos fair in 1748.[12] Succeeding Governor Tomás Véliz Cachupín found that Comanches had already discovered the French trade connection, which diminished their dependence on Taos. During his two administrations (1749-54 and 1762-67), Vélez Cachupín succeeded on two fronts. By offering gifts and military agreements to the Comanches as aid against their traditional enemies, he both curbed their hostilities and laid the groundwork for a Comanche alliance. And by discouraging French trade, he helped eliminate that threat to New Mexico.[13]

In the 1740s, a veteran frontier officer in Nueva Vizcaya, Captain José de Berroterán, complained of problems in that province produced by the policies and procedures of the Reglamento of 1729. Both a shortage of troops and the resultant problems with Tarahumaras particularly concerned him. With the cutback on routine patrols of their mission villages, the Tarahumaras were now abandoning them and "living like pagans" in the craggy ridges and valleys of the sierras.[14] The two-thousand-peso defense budget prohibited pursuing them into their mountain strongholds. Worse yet, Tarahumara renegades allied with the four hundred or more Apache renegades who had recently moved into the Bolsón de Mapimí between Nueva Vizcaya and Coahuila and, led by Mescalero chieftains Ligero and Pascual, began raiding near Parras, Mapimí, and Chihuahua. These well planned raids forced abandonment of many mining centers. According to Captain Berroterán, if the viceroyalty continued to strive for "frugality" in such dangerous times "the robberies, murder, and property loss would continue."[15]

As a solution, Berroterán recommended that his presidio of San Francisco de Conchos be moved north to La Junta de los Ríos Conchos y del Norte and the garrison at Mapimí relocated at the town of Guajoquilla.[16] Considering his suggestions, the viceroyalty issued a formal declaration of war against the hostiles, but did not immediately respond to Berroteran's recommendation. The viceregal government continued to strive for economy, considering other problems in Sinaloa and Sonora more urgent, and ordered Berroterán to conduct a major campaign against the rancherías of Ligero and Pascual. Obviously disappointed, he dispatched Captain José Sánchez de Campillo with twenty-five soldiers and thirty-five Indian auxiliaries to route the Apaches. Little came of this military effort since Ligero and Pascual easily avoided Berroteran's troops in the rough wilderness completely unknown to Captain Sánchez.[17]

During the 1730s and 1740s, Pericues and Guaicurues in Lower California staged two major rebellions. The revolts stemmed from the general poverty of that province, coupled with thievery of the meager food supplies by the occasional English and Dutch pirates, and crewmen of the annual Manila Galleon. In retaliation, the Indians abandoned the religious missions and rebelled. But smallpox, measles, and the addition of a second garrison, San José del Cabo, on the southern tip of the peninsula, finally defeated them. Lower California's Indian population continued to decline, dropping to less than eight thousand by 1760. Except from the point of view of defense against foreign intrusion, Lower California never succeeded as a colonial effort.[18]

In the spring of 1733, Sonora officially became a separate province with Captain Manual Bernal de Huidobro of the old presidio of San Felipe y Santiago de Sinaloa as its first governor. The military situation in Sonora had reached an extremely critical stage. Lower Pimas revolted in 1737, Seris pillaged ranches and mines, and Western Apaches continued their hit-and-run raids. Sonora's presidial forces could not control the hostility without assistance from neighboring provinces. In his campaigning, Governor Huidobro achieved battlefield successes that had eluded him earlier, but campaigns against Seris and Pimas proved greater challenges than the warnings of a coming uprising.[19] The vast expense of sterile desert stretching westward to the Gulf of California worked to the advantage of Indian rebels. So too did the rough barren ranges of the Bacoatzi and Cerro Prieto mountains. Summer heat further aggravated the demands of rugged terrain. Captain Agustín de Vildósola rightly concluded that the Sonora campaigns had been long, hard, and expensive. Many of the troops, particularly the 50 presidials and the 285 indios amigos from Nueva Vizcaya, marched great distances during the revolts and contended with innumerable obstacles.[20]

Immediate causes of the Yaqui Revolt of 1740, part of the chain reaction of rebellions, were floods and famine and widespread looting by Yaquis and other Indians on mission granaries and Spanish properties. Since 1735, a gradual buildup of tensions in the Yaqui community came to a head as miners and hacendados intensified pressure for more Indian labor from the missions, royal officials asserted stronger jurisdiction over civil affairs in the Jesuit missions, and the Yaqui leadership itself, under the direction of Muni and Bernabé, two Indian governors, pressed for fundamental changes in the mission program itself.[21]

Like the Pueblo Rebellion of 1680, the Yaqui Revolt covered a wide geographical area and drew in a significant number of Indian allies. Still, it was not as bloody as the Pueblo affair. Between February-October the Yaquis and their allies sacked, burned, and pillaged haciendas, ranches, mines, and missions, but killed surprisingly few people. At its height, Yaqui rebels, often leaderless, controlled over 100 leagues of territory from Suaqui Grande in the north to San Miguel in the south.

Lasting some six months, the Yaqui Revolt compared to characteristics of the Tarahumara and Pueblo Revolts. Grievances were deep-seated, rooted in excessive demands and expropriation of any Indian surplus. In all three cases, both mission fathers and royal officials abused the Indians. The Yaqui Revolt is different in that no overall command emerged during the armed conflict. Muni and

Bernabé were in Mexico City petitioning the viceroy for relief when the rebellion broke out.[22] The rebellion itself, compared to the Tarahumara revolt, consisted of many localized rebel bands, each with its own leader. When they achieved their purpose, each simply returned to their mission fields or rancherías.

The Jesuits accused secular officials of land grabs and concluded that this is what drove the Indians to rebellion. But the Jesuits were worried about plans expressed by Governor Manual Bernal de Huidobro to turn the missions over to secular priests and integrate the Yaquis into colonial society. After all, the Jesuits had long exhausted the original ten year plan to pacify, civilize and prepare the Yaquis for social integration. In contrast, the Jesuits were arguing that secularization needed to be postponed.[23] Caught in the middle of this political conflict were the Yaquis.

They themselves, under the leadership of Bernabé and Muni, governors of Huírivis and Ráum pueblos, respectively, had their own complaints. These focused around longstanding abuses by certain resident fathers as well as mixed bloods and other Indians from outside the Yaqui missions. Governor Huidobro, no great friend of the Jesuits, heard their complaints in July of 1738 and conducted an investigation of conflicts within the mission program. Bernabé and Muní complained about excessive labor demands by the mission fathers and the shipping of their surplus to the California missions. Their communal properties were being taken away and the mission fathers were preventing them from interacting with Spanish society. Huidobro reacted to their grievances by sending Bernabé and Muní to petition personally before the viceroy in Mexico City. During their absence, the wide-spread plundering began, and when they returned to Yaqui territory this had passed into armed rebellion.

In comparison to Cogoxito, Quautlatas, Teporame, Popé, and Osebaca, Bernabé and Muni did not advocate violence as a solution to Yaqui problems with Spanish society. In fact, they used the system to organize their protests. Both leaders saw the need for some sort of balance of power between the Jesuits and developing Spanish society.[24] Unfortunately, Bernabé and Muni were executed and decapitated on June 23, 1741 by Interim Governor Agustín de Valdósola, their impaled heads circulated in all Yaqui rancherías as a warning to any would be troublemakers.

Like Osebaca of the Tarahumara, Bernabé and Muni were "marginal men," caught in a power play between Jesuit fathers and temporal officials. But they were not confused in their aims; they wanted to preserve the well-organized tax-free mission community with Yaqui grievances responded to, especially the Yaquis' right to their own time, labor, and surplus. But their very position on the bridge of transition between Jesuit missions and secular society was responsible for their failure to appreciate the type of movement which they helped create. With the expulsion of their Jesuit protectors in 1767, Yaqui resistance would take on a new dimension.

Serious as the Yaqui revolt on the northern frontier seemed at the time, it constituted but a prelude to the Seri Revolt of 1749. In this long, drawn-out rebellion over two thousand Seris, allied with Sibubapas, Piatos, Upper Pimas, and

Apaches, rose up against the Spaniards and ravaged Sonora from the Río San Miguel west to the coastal plain and from the lower Sonora River north to the Río Magdalena. The episode sparking the revolt occurred at the mission village of Santa María de Pópulo, where Seri lands belonging to some thirty families were distributed in equal plots among frontier families of the new presidio of San Miguel de Horcasitas (present Horcasitas). When a delegation of Seri leaders and some Pimas facing similar seizure of land protested, their families were rounded up and the women deported to Guatemala and Yucatán. The Seri men, already belligerent over usurpation of their mission lands, now talked threateningly of expelling the Spaniards altogether. Abandoning their settlement, they attacked ranches and mines in the area from Pópulo to the pueblo of Pitic.[25]

To protect the miners and settlers, Sonora's new governor, Lieutenant Colonel Diego Ortiz Parrilla, and his subordinates quickly planned a major offensive against the Seri. An expeditionary force of 75 presidials led by Parrilla and 400 indios amigos led by Pima captain Luis Oacpicagigua began a war of extermination against them in the Cerro Prieto range and on Tiburón Island off the Sonoran coast. The campaign lacked the success indicated in Governor Parrilla's report. The Seris eluded the combat troops who sorted into enemy territory, and the governor managed to capture but a handful of Seris, mostly women and children.[26]

Because the Pima Revolt drew attention away from them in 1751, the unchecked Seri rebels continued to devastate the province, striking as far north as the Bolaños de Plata mine. But in 1753, a Seri delegation negotiated a peace pact, stipulating return of their women and lands. Of course, Governor Pablo Arce y Arroyo could not meet these demands, and Seris continued their ambushes. The next governor of Sonora, Juan Antonio de Mendoza, put together a major offensive in 1755 that struck at the heart of the Cerro Prieto. "In the campaign," remarked the governor, "we surprised the enemy with the beating of drums, put them to flight, and penetrated one of their canyons."[27] In a later offensive, Mendoza was killed by the rebel leader Becerro, himself mortally wounded. On November 7, 1761, Captain Gabriel de Vildósola, leading a column of 420 soldiers, attacked a camp of 200 Seris and managed to slay 49 enemy warriors, capture 63 others (mostly women and children), recover 322 horses and mules, and take a great amount of booty, all without noticeably intimating the Indians. But until the major expeditionary force organized by Inspector General José de Gálvez finally stood up to the ever-restless Seris, their raids continued to sap the morale and strength of Sonoran frontiersmen.[28]

Still, the Upper Pima Revolt of Luis Oacpicagigua climaxed the whole series of popular uprisings in Sonora. The rebellions expressed the Indian animosity immediately stimulated by particular abuses in the exercise of secular/religious authority, and from 1684 to 1749, occasional unorganized uprisings erupted in successive areas. But like the Pueblo rebellion, the Pima Revolt benefited from the leadership of one man. On the morning of November 20, 1751, the Indian governador of Sáric, Luis Oacpicagigua, convened Indian leaders in one of the small valleys near that mission community located close to the source of the Río Altar. There, like the Pueblo and Tarahumara rebellions, they planned a general conspiracy with the expressed objectives of suppression of Spanish society and a return to Indian lifeways. The territory Luis of Sáric desired to liberate was bordered by the Magdalena and Altar river valleys in the south, the Gulf of California in the west, the Gila Valley in the north, and the San Pedro Valley in the east, some fifty thousand square miles of arid and semi-arid basin and range country.[29] Specifically, the Spaniards and Jesuits were to be driven from Pimería Alta, and neither life nor property was to be spared.[30]

Tribesmen only in the sense that they spoke various dialects of the same language, the several Upper Pima groups had distinct cultural differences. In the east, they lived in rancherías, while nomadic bands roamed the northwest, living as food gathers in the more isolated part of Pimería Alta. The Pimas recognized no central authority and, though several rancherías cohered somewhat in ceremonial life and through kinship ties, unity for any purpose other than warfare did not exist. Political cooperation never joined more than fifteen hundred people throughout Pimería Alta. Similar to the Yaqui Revolt, the insurrection had to trigger the support of some fifteen thousand scattered people. Luis Oacpicagigua displayed extraordinary daring and resourcefulness in encouraging others to unite in rebellion, and he should be honored for trying to join his people under such discouraging circumstances.

Luis began to revolt by murdering eighteen Spanish residents he enticed into entering his house at Sáric. The missionary Father Juan Nentvig, alerted by Father Jacobo Sedelmayr, escaped to Tubutama where the two of them, along with several soldiers, organized the other refugees for a defense of the mission. Luis and about 125 warriors attacked the mission, set fire to the building, but failed to flush out the defenders. After dark, the beleaguered refugees sneaked past an Indian picket and fled southward, abandoning two seriously wounded soldiers.[31] At the Caborca and Sonoita outposts, missionaries Tomás Tello and Enrique Ruben were less fortunate; both were killed. The rebellion extended eastward to San Ignacio, Remedios, and Magdalena, and over one hundred pobladores met death in the violence. Though some attacks occurred at the Santa Cruz River mission of San Xavier del Bac and Tumacacori, no other missionaries were killed. Within three months this phase of the revolt ended, almost as quickly as it began.[32]

The Pima Revolt found causes in disputes over land and labor. Like previous revolts, roots of the revolt were in the conflicting interests between frontier economic interests. Another difficulty lay in the mission fathers' inability to recognize and deal wisely with Indian leadership. These problems began somewhat earlier, for changes and stresses had occurred in Upper Pima country for quite some time. Organization of the religious mission changed considerably with the assignment in 1732 of three foreign missionaries, led by Ignacio Xavier Keller, to the new frontier outposts of Santa María Soamca, Guevavi, and San Xavier del Bac. After departure of their military escort, these fathers depended on the captain-protector system for their personal safety and success of their mission program. In the past, the missions played only small parts in congregating and settling the Pimas, but now the Indians faced a rude awakening.[33]

By the mid-1740s, the Jesuits strengthened their position in Pimería Alta, settling about half the tribe near urban centers or religious missions. Overseen by Indian captains and under strict obligation, the Indians spent two days a week cultivating revenue-producing lands. The missionaries then sold these agricultural products to local miners, ranchers, or other vecinos. In this way, Ignacio Keller and the other Jesuits hoped to make the mission communities self-sufficient. To stimulate this administrative change they also actively influenced the selection of Indian leadership.[34]

With the increased economic and political activities came a trend toward more contact with mestizo and casta vecinos. This occurred partly because the opening of neighboring ranches and farms affected the Pimas through introduction of private enterprise. A labor draft allowed local vecinos a quota of Indian laborers in their fields and ranches, which meant that part of the mission's population was absent during the important harvest season. Assessing the number of Pimas affected by this policy is difficult, but presumably it was sizeable. Also Spanish colonists drawn to Pimería Alta to take advantage of squatter's rights there further pressured the Indians by their steady encroachment on the ill-defined lands traditionally laid out as mission ejidos. As mixed-blood squatters preempted the best river-bottom acres, Indian resentment increased.[35]

With the arrival of the new governor, Diego Ortiz Parrilla, mission protection of Pimas from outsiders was gradually usurped by temporal authority. In addition to this threat to Jesuit interests, the change of authority seriously affected the Pimas' ability to retain control of their own village lands, especially if the greed of royal officials in any way represented Spain's more ordinary citizens. In contrast to the 1730s when Pimas based their strength on the ability to negotiate, Upper Pimas by 1750 found themselves threatened by loss of land and local autonomy. Now stripped of bargaining status, Pimas watched as an economic self-interest become even more restrictive and overpowering.[36]

On March 18, 1752, Luis Oacpicagigua surrendered to Captain José Díaz del Carpio. Of course, he blamed the mission fathers for inciting revolt, accusing the Jesuits of using revenue-producing lands for their own benefits and of ordering the whipping of those who questioned their fattening of mission coffers. Luis also testified that most mixed blood land managers overly oppressed the Indians. Governor Parrilla sympathized with Luis, filed a favorable report, then allowed him to return home. He declared a peace and planned to leave for Horcasitas, but royal orders delayed his departure. Upon receipt of conflicting opinions, viceregal officials ordered an extensive investigation into the causes of the Pima Revolt. But Parrilla's report received approval, and the viceroy, the first Conde de Revillagedo, highly recommended him to succeeding Viceroy Marqués de las Amarillas.[37]

In 1753, Parrillas' replacement, Pablo Arce Y Arroyo, conducted a thorough investigation of the revolt. But as Governor Arce y Arroyo gathered testimonies vindicting the Jesuits and implicating Parrilla, the Pimas made mockery of the negotiated peace. The revolt continued. Pima warriors began hit-and-run warfare, and rumors had it that Luis of Sáric planned another uprising. In May of 1753, Luis Oacpicagigua and one of his principal lieutenants, Luis of Pitic, were summoned for questioning. After intensive interrogation, both leaders attempted suicide in their prison cells. The attempt failed and as a prisoner of the governors of Sonora, Luis Oacpicagigua died early in 1755 while languishing in the Horcasitas jail.[38]

But Pima resistance did not end with Luis Oacpicagigua's death. For some twenty years, the Upper Pimas, Seris, and their Tiburón kinsmen waged a guerrilla war difficult to suppress. As Spanish vecinos became more dismayed, demoralized, and debilitated, the Indians increased their resistance. Such success attracted Pápago, Piato, Sobáipuri, and Seri recruits, and their warrior numbers rapidly multiplied. Pimería Alta became an amalgam of various people operating in military strategy with a cunning warfare that shook the Sonora frontier. To cope with this spreading hostility, the viceroy established two new presidios in the 1750s. Each was to be garrisoned with fifty troops and stationed near mission settlements in the far north. To check Seri resistance, a third new fort was established in 1765 at San Carlos de Buenavista on the lower reaches of the Río Yaqui.[39]

Still, the prime causes of the Pima Revolt was that abuses and exploitation had become an unacceptable pattern on Indian life in Sonora. Sporadic irritant problems can be isolated, but they lack causal implications. The reason for this pattern of accommodation's sudden unacceptability to the Indian is difficult to pinpoint, especially since missionary activity did not automatically give rise to insurrection. An equally important question concerning the revolt is why the conspirators chose to rise in concerted rebellion when guerrilla warfare seemed a more viable alternative. The answer is found in the frequent instances of mission humiliations, thwarting of legitimate Indian grievances, excessive land encroachment, by ranchers, vecinos, and Sonoran mining development, especially as applied to the use of Indian labor.

But among the Pimas, no separatist sentiment existed to which Luis Oacpicagigua and his lieutenants could appeal. Sobáipuri kinsmen, when asked for warriors, commonly rejected the request and if they did provide men, usually commanded their own contingent. Indians served in the revolt for no more consideration than lodging and a share of the plunder. According to a veteran presidio commander, some Sobáipuris and Pimas of the upper Santa Cruz River area simply did not want to fight, preferring to make the best of conditions in mission villages or as day-labor near the many productive mining camps. Also, Indians near the presidios of Coredoguachi (alias Fronteras) and San Felipe de Guevavi (alias Terrenate) frequently joined presidials as indios amigos against people of their own race.[40]

Strikingly, the one outstanding similarity among most Indian conspirators is their connection to the Jesuit missions. Luis Oacpicagigua's major lieutenant Jabanimó, represented a growing group of religious leaders who remained hostile to missionary influence and who felt bitterly antagonistic toward the erection of whipping posts and appointments and bestowals of canes of office from missionary visitors. In contrast to Jabanimó, Luis had left the missionaries' sphere of influence and consequentially, had regular militia approval and esteem. Governor Parrilla considered him an exceptional military leader, influential among the Upper Pimas. Parrilla even honored him with the title "Captain General of the Pimas" for his role in leading indios amigos during the Seri Revolt. Luis fully appreciated his oratorical abilities and the diplomatic esteem accorded him by his followers.[41] These two Indian men, lacking a central leadership but provoked to action by similar forces, both became leaders inclined toward Indian unity. Not embattled tribal leaders, ignorant of frontier society in the far north, these two charismatic leaders knew in detail both mission and temporal aspects of frontier society.[42]

The Pima Revolt marked the emergence of a forceful spokesman for those angered and discontented Pimas now lacking a local ranchería community to give them an effective voice. But these Indians, whether detribalized by entry into missions or into civilian militia, saw no reason to accept the direction and discipline of a single leader. Though sensitive enough to realize the extent of his people's dissatisfaction, Luis Oacpicagigua failed to weigh accurately their malcontent against the compensating benefits of Spanish society. Despite their drawbacks, missions, mines, presidios, and urban centers offered advantages obvious to many Pimas whose support he needed. Perhaps Luis underestimated the deadening force of sheer inertia on many Pimas. He certainly assumed too readily that Pima suspicion and hatred concentrated solely on the mission fathers.[43] Still, the revolt marked the beginnings of Pima acknowledgement that the future offered more than helpless acceptance of whatever Jesuit paternalism provided. From the revolt, a new leadership surfaced, equipped with an example of action, a method of implementation, and, most importantly, a martyr.

The question now becomes: What did the Pima Revolt have in common with other northern uprisings? Was it Pima resentment over the direct use of natural and human resources with its vexed question of Indian rights? It is apparent that Indian resistance was in part a reaction to economic changes as the territory developed--as when, for instance, a ranchería people were affected more by appropriations of land and alien control of the rivers than by soil erosion and absolute lack of water. Nevertheless, the matter of control involving a complicated superstructure of government inducements within a deteriorating environment is given undue prominence in analysis of the revolts. Every Indian reaction to the introduction of European regulation and expansion has had some reference to questions of land or labor;[44] but in the Pima Revolt, that factor unduly obscures many elements of particular significance: the attempts to organize the Pimas under the leadership of Indians who had already dipped deeply into Spanish society; and the intertribal outlook and emergence of new men as Indian leaders.

The Pima Revolt is comparable to the revolts of the Tepehuán, Tarahumaras and Seris in that missionaries never extended influence over the whole nation, but here the comparison stops. Mission work among the Seris met periodic, unlocalized resistance for one hundred years, and the violent guerrilla warfare gave way to peace only after "crime-committing" rebels were exterminated. Seri resistance was similar to the Pima. In both cases, about half the tribe remained beyond the mission influence of shaping Indians to the new order, but even so, there seemed to be a demand for missionaries, or at least for their system of "tribute-free" protection.

The Pima Revolt, like the Pueblo, Tarahumara, Tepehuán, and Yaqui uprisings, suffered from an Indian leadership that disintegrated or was eliminated after the initial success. In contrast to Luis Oacpicagigua, Popé, Ignacio Osebaca, and Quautlatas were religious leaders with great tribal influence, and their success is largely attributable to that intertribal influence. Indeed, as religious leaders, they could more easily coordinate tribal interactions where there had been none before.

Their effective use of religious influence makes them truly impressive Indian leaders. But that influence was short-lived. It was apparent nonetheless that there was a widespread communication among northern Indian leaders.

The Pima Revolt failed because of its too close identification with Luis Oacpicagigua. His bond of personal friendship being the only uniting force he could offer his followers meant that his influence extended only over those leaders who lacked other social, religious, or economic ties. This weakness might have been deduced from the relative isolation of the missions before 1700, but it only became apparent when tested by the demands of the 1751 uprising, and military authorities recognized it could be employed deliberately in suppressing the revolt. Luis also failed to assess realistically the general conditions in Pimería Alta. He mistakenly took complaints and views of other leaders suffering under the Spanish economy as acceptance of his attack on the situation. The unstable alliance he assembled from the Indian coalition that drifted to his independent solution broke up when he surrendered. Similar to the Yaquis Bernabé and Muni, personal force removed from the alliance, Indian unity reverted to localized hit-and-run raiding.

The rest of the Indian leadership, those who remained within Pima society by choice, found their authority challenged by the Spaniards, who at the same time were working away at their economic base and political autonomy. These Indian leaders, then, retreated into the common mass of Pima society. The appearance of few colonial chieftains of a group called captain-generals creates some confusion over the post-Luis history of the Pima leadership. Perhaps the lessons of maintaining a separate identity and thus escaping the burdens imposed by the Spaniards, were jealously guarded because of what happened to Luis Oacpicagigua.

CHAPTER V

FOOTNOTES

[1]Pedro de Rivera's report and recommendations are published in Vito Alessio Robles, ed., Diario y derrotero de lo caminado, visto y observado in la visita que hizo a los presidios de la Nueva España Septentrional el Brigadier don Pedro de Rivera (Mexico, 1946).

[2]Reglamento para todos los presidios de las provincias internas de esta Governación, . . .Hecho por el Excmo. Señor Marqués de Casa-Fuerte, Vi-Rey, Governador, y Capitan General de estos Reynos (Mexico, 1729), Articles 154-95. For a copy, see AGI, Guadalajara 144; the text appears in Robles, Diario y derrotero, 199-234.

[3]Viceroy Marques de Casafuerte to the Real Hacienda, Mexico, May 3, 1723, AGI Guadalajara 171; Expediente sobre la conquista . . .de indios de . . . la Nueva Vizcaya, años de 1723 y 1724, AGI, Guadalajara 171.

[4]Since the rough country around the Bolsón de Mapimí offered but bare subsistence from game and edible flora as mescal and berries, Indians stole without compunction from the scarcely less poverty-ridden civilians. The guerrilla warfare at which Apaches excelled became but a means to an end as thievery gained importance. With predictable regularity, from out of the Bolsón, raiders desolated the Valle de San Buenaventura, Santa Rosa, and Monclova in Coahuila.

[5]Moorhead, The Apache Frontier, 170-74, 200-204.

[6]Rupert H. Richardson, The Comanche Barrier to the South Plains Settlement, 18-21, 53; Newcomb, The Indians of Texas, 155-91.

[7]Alfred B. Thomas, ed., The Plains Indians and New Mexico, 1751-1778: A Collection of Documents Illustrative of the History of the Eastern Frontier of New Mexico, 17-18, 25-36, 58-59.

[8]Proclamación del governador Juan Domingo de Bustamante, Santa Fe, September 17, 1725, SANM, doc. 340.

[9]Criminal proceedings against seven gente de razón, Santa Fe, August 3-September 7, 1726, SANM, doc. 340a; Proclamacion del Governador Enrique de Olvide y Michelina, Santa Fe, January 7, 1737, SANM, doc. 414.

[10]Thomas, The Plains Indians and New Mexico, 7, 17-18, 91-92.

[11]Proclamacion del governador Gaspar de Mendoza, Santa Fe, March 21, 1741, SANM, doc. 438; Proclamacion del governador Joaquín Codallos y Rabal, Santa Fe, May 30, 1774, SANM, doc. 455.

[12]Codallos y Rabal, Proclamacion, Santa Fe, February 14, 1746, SANM, doc. 495; Ralph E. Twitchell, The Spanish Archives of New Mexico, 2:227.

13Thomas, The Plains Indians and New Mexico, 25-38, 57-58. See also Herbert E. Bolton's "French Intrusions into New Mexico, 1749-1752," in John Francis Bannon, Bolton and the Spanish Borderlands, 150-71.

14Captain José de Berroterán to Viceroy Conde de Revillagigedo, Informe, Mexico, April 17, 1748 (certified copy in 84 articles), article 10, AGI, Guadalajara 513. This informe is reproduced in Documentos-Mexico, 1:161-224.

15Ibid., articles 56,84.

16Ibid., articles 81-83.

17Diario de la campaña executado de orden del Exmo. Señor Conde de Revillagigedo . . ., Mexico, September 25, 1749 (certified copy enclosed with Bucareli to Arriaga, No. 870, Mexico, April 26, 1773), AGI, Guadalajara 513.

18Testimonio sobre la sublevación de los indios en La Isla de Californias, y cartas del governador Manual Bernal de Huidobro . . ., Mexico, April 3, 1937, AGI, Guadalajara 135; Peter Masten Dunne, Black Robes in Lower California (Berkeley, 1952), pp. 377-78, 404; Marguerite Eyler Wilbur, ed., The Indian Uprising in Lower California, 1734-1737, as Described by Father Sigismundo Taravajal.

19On the Yaqui Revolt, see Luis Navarro García, La Sublevación Yaqui de 1740, and Evelyn Hu-DeHart, Missionaries, Miners, and Indians.

20Agustín de Vildósola to Viceroy Duque de la Conquista, Sinaloa, March 17, 1741, AGI, Guadalajara 301.

21Hu DeHart, Missionaries, Miners, and Indians, 59-60.

22Ibid., 66-68.

23Ibid., 76-79.

24Ibid., 66-67.

25Testimonio de cartas. . .sobre la sublevación Seri, Mexico, January 28, 1750, AGI, Guadalajara 188.

26Autos a consulta del governador de Sinaloa, Don Diego Ortiz de Parrilla..., Mexico, 1757 (enclosed as 290 folios), fols. 128, 228, AGI Guadalajara 137.

27Juan Antonio de Mendoza to Pedro Anselmo Sánchez de Tagle, Horcasitas, February 15, 1757, AGI, Guadalajara 301.

28Navarro García, Don José de Gálvez, 86-87; Tamarón, Demostración, 284.

[29]Kessell, Friars, Soldiers, and Reformers, 3.

[30]For a standard treatment of the revolt, see Russell C. Ewing, "The Pima Uprising, 1751-1752: A Study in Spain's Indian Policy," unpublished Ph.D. dissertation, University of California, Berkeley, 1934; and his "The Pima Outbreak in November, 1751," NMHR 8 (1938): 337-46; and "The Pima Uprising of 1751," in Greater America: Essays in Honor of Herbet E. Bolton, 259-80.

[31]Testimonio . . .sobre los Pimas Altas en la provincia de Sonora, Horcasitas, November 23, 1753, AGI, Guadalajara 419.

[32]Ibid.

[33]Russell C. Ewing, "Investigations into the Causes of the Pima Uprising of 1751," Mid-America 23 (April 1941): 138-51.

[34]John L. Kessell, Mission of Sorrows: Jesuit Guevavi and the Pimas, 1691-1767, 105-49.

[35]Ibid.

[36]Before the revolt, irritating conflicts between Governor Parrilla and Father Keller festered over the political affairs of mission administration. Parrilla accused Keller of usurping authority in military operations. Father Keller perhaps was unduly jealous of Parrilla's assumption of authority in his district; he certainly resented the governor's sharp criticism of Jesuit administration. Ignacio Keller to Captain Juan Antonio Menocal, Soamca, November 28, 1751; Parrilla, Decree, San Ignacio. March 24, 1752, AGI, Guadalajara 419.

[37]Luis Oacpicagigua, Declaración, San Ignacio, March 25, 1752, AGI Guadalajara 419; Parrilla to Viceroy Revillagigedo, San Ignacio, December 1, 1751, AGI, Guadalajara 418. To answer charges that Jesuits were responsible for the revolt, Keller traveled to Mexico City where on August 25, 1752, he prepared a "Consulta" refuting the charges. In it, he placed full responsibility for the revolt on Governor Parrilla. Documentos-Mexico, 4th series, 1:28.

[38]Pablo Arce y Arryo, Testimonios, Horcasitas, November, 1753-January, 1754, AGI, Guadalajara 418.

[39]Moorhead, The Presidio, 52.

[40]Captain Fernando Sánchez Salvador to Consejo de Indias, Sonora, July 7, 1752, AGI, Guadalajara 418; Governor Juan de Piñeda to Viceroy Marqués de Cruillas, Mexico, May 2,1776, AGI, Guadalajara 416.

[41]But according to Jesuit historian Francisco Javier Alegre, Luis openly stirred sedition among his people and constantly complained about the Jesuits to anyone willing to listen. See Francisco Javier Alegre, S.J., Historia de la Compañía de Jesus en Nueva Espana, 3:289-91.

[42]Accusations by Governor Parrilla, and Luis Oacpicaguigua, are in Testimonio . . . sobre la sublevación de los pueblos de la Pimería Alta, Mexico, January 31, 1765, and Testimonio . . . de autos formados contra Don Juan Antonio Menocal, Mexico, February 11, 1754, AGI, Guadalajara 419.

[43]Miguel Quijano, solicitor of the Jesuit province of New Spain, Informe, Documentos-Mexico, 1: 33-57; and Declaraciónes (twenty-six from frontier residents and fourteen from Pimas), Ures, November 23, 1754, AGI, Guadalajara 419.

[44]José Ignacio Gallegos, Durango Colonial, 1536-1821, 77.

CHAPTER VI

THE REORGANIZATION
OF PRESIDIO DEFENSES: A
RESPONSE TO THE INDIOS BARBAROS

The 1763 Treaty of Paris ending the Seven Years' War eliminated the French threat on the North American mainland and forced Spain to cede Florida to Great Britain. In exchange, Spain received Havana and Manila, occupied by the British during the war. The treaty removed French control from the Mississippi, moved New Spain's northern boundary east and England's boundary west of that great river. A Spanish-owned Louisiana now protected Texas from European threats, but the Bourbon empire quickly learned that elimination of the French replaced one problem with another: New Spain now had aggressive English colonies as neighbors. Meanwhile, Bourbon officials argued that the time was long overdue for the missions to be secularized and their Indian populations integrated into colonial society. Suddenly, in 1767, the Jesuits were expelled from New Spain.

As internal tensions within Spain's American colonies and political maneuvering in Europe prevented a consistent Bourbon policy for America, Charles III dispatched General Juan de Villaba to New Spain with orders to bolster its sagging defenses, create a regular army, and raise a formal corps of provincial militia. Sent as part of this mission, Visitor General José de Gálvez was to reorganize the administrative and economic machinery of the viceroyalty. Royal appointee Marqués de Rubí, a field marshal commissioned to inspect thoroughly defenses in the Provicias Internas, spent two years there, gathering material for his celebrated assessment of frontier military organization. The report was largely the work of Nicolás de Lafora, his captain of royal engineers, whose 1771 detailed map comprehensively surveyed the northern frontier.[1]

Rubí's lengthy report suggested more startling changes. Distinguishing clearly between land Spain actually occupied in the Provincias Internas and imaginary territory under her control, he proposed a single outer line of fixed-post defenses along the thirteenth parallel. The line would run from the Gulf of California to the Gulf of Mexico, some 1,715 miles of irregular terrain. According to Rubi, this required only fifteen presidios, spaced about one hundred miles apart. Each presidio company, 50 men, including 3 officers and a sergeant, could communicate readily with the nearest garrison to the east and west, support its operations when necessary, and patrol half the intermediate terrain on either side. North of the line would remain two presidios which because of their isolation required reinforcement by larger companies of 80 men each. These two garrisons were Santa Fe in New Mexico and San Antonio in Texas. Others would be suppressed or more strategically located in conformity with the fixed line. Rubí also proposed construction of six new forts along the Río Grande to close a gap in the line between El Paso and San Juan Bautista. This system of fortified villages supported by a force of a thousand men constantly shifting in response to changing threats sent logistical costs skyrocketing, but provided effective protection to settlements, mines, and travel routes. Hounded by a crown crying for reduced expenditures, military officials desperately sought some economic alternative like the Rubí plan.[2]

Flaws in the Rubí recommendations arose mainly because the presidios were in fixed locations. To be truly effective, such a presidial chain needed to be comprehensive enough to cover all potential trouble spots and securely enough held to permit immediate implementation of force sufficient to meet probable contingencies. A military force of 910 officers and men, with other responsibilities as well, could not prevent incursions of Indian hostiles. Nor could it man seventeen presidios with effective garrisons, much less the economic factors of the effort. Still, the Reglamento of 1772, sanctioned by Spain, implemented Rubí's proposals for this supposedly impregnable chain of frontier defenses, and enforced his recommendations to reduce military expenditures. Based on his report, the Reglamento provided for immediate appointment of a commandant inspector to coordinate the program, and for eventual appointment of a commandant general.[3]

When Rubí began his celebrated tour of the Provincias Internas, Visitor General Gálvez remained in the viceregal capital to supervise efforts for effective occupation of Upper California and suppression of Seri, Pima, and Sibubapa rebels. General Gálvez raised some 300,000 pesos from private and public sources, recruited an army, and constructed two brigantines to transport his Sonora Expedition up the west coast of New Spain. Sailing north from San Blas to establish a base at La Paz, Lower California, for expeditions to strengthen the defenses of the Pacific coast, Gálvez ordered Colonel Domingo Elizondo to land at Guaymas and begin military operations against Indian rebels in Sonora. Soon he had about one thousand men in the field. From March-May, Elízondo unsuccessfully pursued Indian rebels in the Bacoatzi mountains, the Cerro Prieto range, and on Tiburón Island.[4]

Elizondo warred less against Seri rebels--they probably mustered no more than three hundred fighting men--than he did against one of the most rugged wildernesses in northern Mexico. Towering mountain peaks loom over deep narrow canyons, making the Cerro Prieto and Bacoatzis imposing enemies. Campaigns into them by Juan de Mendoza, Gabriel de Vildósola, Juan Bautista de Anza, and Colonel Elizondo, although netting some Indian deaths and recovering various amounts of booty, failed miserably. "It is an inhospitable terrain," reported Elizondo, "an incomprehensible maze of mountains, independent of one another, that rise and fall into deep canyons and sheer ridges."[5]

Late in March of 1769, three divisions of infantry and presidials numbering about two hundred men each, took the field from Guaymas and Pitic. Two under Colonel Elizondo penetrated the Cerro Prieto from the north, while the other under Captain Lorenzo Cancio Sierra y Ciénfuegos marched in from the south. The two forces would supposedly meet, but Cancio's troops, exhausted from the forced march, could mount no offensive. In the Cajón de la Cara Pintada, Elizondo' s

PRESIDIAL SOLDIER

troops met some scattered Seri resistance, but suffering the same problem as Cancio's could not pursue. With this military situation, the command regrouped and marched back to Guaymas and Pitic. Once again the elements defeated the king's forces.[6]

Bourbon authorities ordered full support to the California expedition being organized on the peninsula. From La Paz, Gálvez returned to the mainland in May of 1769, to assume command in Sonora and once there issued a proclamation of general amnesty and economic assistance to all rebels who made peace within forty days. Thirty-two Seri families responded to the offer, but discovered that instead of amnesty and welfare, they would receive internment at Pitic or service as military allies against their own kinsmen. The visitor general, after another offer of general amnesty, began an all-out military campaign. Fugitives were to be rounded up once and for all so he could continue the more important business of economic expansion.[7]

In October of 1769, a thoroughly disillusioned Gálvez arrived in Pitic and made a vigorous but unrewarding assault on the Indian stronghold of Cerro Prieto. Meanwhile, because troops had been pulled from Sonoran garrisons, Apaches increased their attacks there and in Nueva Vizcaya. Seriously ill and depressed over the failure of his Sonoran campaign, Gálvez retired to bed, and his command went to Colonel Elizondo who after one final offensive, reduced operations to punitive harassment of the ever-restless Seris, Sibubapas, and Pimas.[8]

Failure of the Sonora campaign, coupled with the spread of rebellion into Nueva Vizcaya, prompted Bourbon officials to conclude that it served no purpose to continue a military offensive in one region while the rest of the frontier virtually flamed with revolt. Preferring defensive action only in critical areas, military advisors in Madrid suggested to the king that frontier officials attempt to appease the Seri and Pima hostiles with gifts and food rations. Gálvez had directed his attention to this problem, and his recommendations laid the groundwork for yet another military tactic of punitive expeditions, trade alliances, and reliance on indios amigos (Indian auxiliaries).[9] But formulating effective tactics proved a difficult task. The vast northern wilderness, characterized by diverse topography and ecology, played havoc with the Sonora expedition. The Bourbons recognized that economic reorganization could not occur if they were losing the Indian war. Toward this end, royal officials meticulously studied the Rubí recommendations.

In September of 1771, a royal appointee of exceptional ability and energy, Antonio María Bucareli, replaced the Marqués de Croix as the forty-sixth viceroy of New Spain. Ordered to proceed with the policy of economic development and settlement of the Indian problem, Bucareli moved with well-placed caution at first. Rumors of a lucrative gold strike in Sonora implied various attendant troubles, and Nueva Vizcaya's Governor José de Fayni issued a report, based on testimony from two mission fathers passing through Durango from Sonora, that Seri and Pima warriors now terrorized that province. Complicating the situation in Sonora, Gileños increased invasions there, and Tarahumara renegades also extended their raids into the eastern portion of the province. These activities waylaid implementation of the planned economic expansion into the Gila River basin, and made maintenance of settlements in Upper California considerably risky. The Rubí recommendations of 1768, as formulated by Visitor General Gálvez and promulgated provisionally by the Marqués de Croix before he left office, now took force.[10]

Hugo O'Conor, experienced frontiersman and lieutenant colonel in Spain's royal army, assumed military responsibility for grappling with renegade Indians. O'Conor spent six years as commandant inspector in an era of transition that manifested little toward final settlement of Indian hostilities. Lieutenant Colonel O'Conor established headquarters in Nueva Vizcaya, toured the frontier, and relied on essentially large-scale military campaigns only slightly modified by special conditions of the presidio function.[11] O'Conor also pursued a policy that combined a concentrated defensive line with strategically located compañías volantes (mobile companies), which proved satisfactory. Presidios dispersed along the line, both too few and too weak, presented no effective defense. Their offensive campaigns, generally failures, cost time and further weakened the line. Governmental officials criticized the strategy, asserting that presidials were no match for Indians who traveled lightly and swiftly, and who, when pressed, scattered to rendezvous later.[12] But meeting Indian renegades on their own terms, especially with mobile companies, proved effective.

O'Conor constructed his chain of frontier fortifications, but Indian warriors readily adjusted to the new fixed-post defenses. Fully aware of weakness in the chain, they easily avoided roving patrols. But a compañía volante criss-crossing Indian terrain could stop attacks or ambushes. To raid a settlement, Indians had to worry about the patrol. They learned to respect the compañía volante since its mobility posed some threat to their raids. Lieutenant Antonio Felix Sánchez previously reported to the governor of Nueva Vizcaya: "The enemies' hit-and-run tactics catch us completely off guard, but if we placed small detachments of troops at the areas which they strike most, and waited for them to attack again, we would be quite successful in defeating them."[13]

Contrasting the fixed presidial company, the compañía volante, from its station at a pueblo or village, patrolled the roads, guarded caravans, and chased hostile bands penetrating the presidio line. But the concept contained some flaws: it assumed that vecinos would not overspread the northern lands, and though presumably operating in concert with presidials, the compañías suffered handicaps that often negated their effectiveness. To function well, the compañía volante program required a manpower increase of a magnitude unacceptable to the viceroyalty. Still, O'Conor managed to implement operation of a mobile company in the early 1770s; he manned it with four hundred veteran dragoons from Mexico and Spain and three hundred recently recruited provincial settler-stockmen types, plus indios amigos.[14]

O'Conor's first general report to the viceroy characterized the state of the Provincias Internas as extremely critical. In just two months, Indian rebels killed forty-five people (mostly vecinos), wounded twenty-one, captured an undetermined number of women and children, burned mission, ranches, and farms, and stole more than a thousand horses and mules. O'Conor acknowledged the Indians' expertise in guerrilla warfare but believed that with creation of new presidios and increased troop strength the situation could be reversed.[15] Spanish residents felt otherwise, and angry tension further strained relations between them and military officials. Governor Fayni vigorously sided with the frontier settlers and reported that Nueva Vizcaya, already suffering a serious economic crisis, could not finance any augmentation of defenses. As an alternative, he recommended immediate short-range defensive measures to placate the civilians.[16]

Viceroy Bucareli responded by convening a war council in March of 1772. At this council, Bucareli underscored the urgency of reorganizing the economic well-being of Nueva Vizcaya and improving fixed-post defenses with minimum logistic expense. He cautiously advocated adherence to the Rubí recommendations for realigning the presidios and suggested that increasing troop strength at the Chihuahua garrison by 300 men would stop Indian hostilities and insure Nueva Vizcaya's safety.[17]

In late June of 1772, Indian hostilities in Sonora, Nueva Vizcaya, Coahuila, and New Mexico increased. A large force of Eastern Apaches conducted a punishing raid near Chihuahua, capturing some 400 horses and killing 5 people, then escaping safely because the garrison lacked mounts with which to give chase. In one day alone, Lipán Apaches in Coahuila killed 23 people, captured 22, and took 954 head of stock. The warfare spread, and Governor Jacobo Ugarte y Loyola protested the use of Rubi's strategies, arguing that realignment of San Sabá, Santa Rosa, and Monclova only weakened the province. New Mexican Governor Pedro Fermín de Mendinueta reported similar problems with the Comanches, expressing fear that spring's arrival would prompt an increase in the intensity and daring of their attacks, and he urged congregating the widely-scattered vecinos into fortified towns. Bucareli rejected the recommendation on economic grounds, suggesting instead construction of a garrison at Taos. Unfortunately, the plan was never acted upon.[18]

Renewed violence in Texas forced viceregal attention. Governor Barón de Riperdá negotiated peace treaties with several Coahuiltecan and Caddoan bands, but in the winter of 1772, he heard rumors that Apaches, Tejas, and Bidais, now allied, were increasing hit-and-run raids in the province. Also, it was rumored that the Nations of the North were amassing firearms from English traders and French now under Spanish rule in Natchitoches. If Riperdá took a hardline approach to the recent hostilities, he ran the risk of open rebellion, which would disastrously affect the Apache alliance. The viceroy cautioned Riperdá to guard against the formation of friendships between the Apaches and Norteños, and make every effort to attract Coahuiltecan and Caddoans into the missions.[19]

Commandant Inspector O'Conor concentrated his efforts on the fixed-post defenses, but responsibility for establishment of defenses beyond the presidial line in Texas and New Mexico fell to provincial governors. Riperdá's formidable task included suppressing the presidios of Los Adaes and Orcoquisac, ordering abandonment of their unprotected missions, reinforcing San Antonio and La Bahía, and settling a detachment of troops in Arroyo de Cíbola. New Mexican Governor Mendinueta's task entailed reinforcement of the garrison of Santa Fe and establishment of a detachment of militiamen at Robledo. But the areas of greatest unrest lay beyond the chain of frontier defenses, and though Riperdá achieved an uneasy peace with the Nations of the North, Mendinueta witnessed unabating attacks by Comanches, Gileños, and Navajos.[20] It is important to note that even when confronting all this large-scale resistance, the crown was not giving up on the northern provinces.

New Mexican settlers fought back, winning some impressive victories over the hated Comanche. In September of 1774, some six hundred soldiers, militiamen and Pueblo amigos led by Indian captain, Carlos Fernández, routed the Comanches in a series of major campaigns. Despite such defeats, the Comanches returned the next year, terrorizing the province and forcing abandonment of many outlying settlements.[21] Viceroy Bucareli sympathized with the situation of New Mexicans, but urged O'Conor first to complete the fixed-post defenses and concentrate on eliminating Apache hostility in Coahuila and Nueva Vizcaya.

In carrying out his orders, O'Conor discovered that most hit-and-run raids on Nueva Vizcaya and Coahuila originated in the Bolsón de Mapimí, mainly from the rancherías of Apache leaders Ligero and Pascual. The most often attacked settlement areas were Cerro Cordo, Mapimí, Parras, El Gallo, and Monclova. Ayudante Mayor Juan de San Vicente reported hostile activities around Chihuahua the worst since the Natagées had negotiated a peace with the commandant inspector.[22]. In March of 1773, with O'Conor out of the area searching for new presidio sites, 300 Indian warriors laid siege to the Janos presidio while others raided nearby settlements. In just a few days, the Indians killed 30 vecinos and wounded or took as prisoner many more. The mission fathers believed that unfaithful Tarahumara renegades were involved in the attacks. No matter how strong their mission program, the Franciscans, who replaced the ousted Jesuits, could not stop Indians from abandoning their mission villages and joining other renegades of the Sierra de Rosario stronghold. They were counted as 1,700 warriors mixed of Tarahumaras, Cholomos, coyotes, lobos, and other castas, led by an Indian named Calaxtrin, his son, and a mestizo named Antonio de la Campa.[23]

In the summer of 1773, local civil officials in Nueva Vizcaya pressured Viceroy Bucareli to do something about the Tarahumaras and the "villainous castas" living among them.[24] Royal officials attributed raids and ambushes around Valle de Santiago, Papasqueiaro, and the pueblo of San Juan del Río to small bands of Tarahumara renegades. They believed friendship with the generally honest, hard-working Tarahumaras was essential for without their military aid the marauding Apaches would remain at large. Reports from Chihuahua pointed to an Apache-Tarahumara alliance that devastated the Cerro Gordo area and the landed estates of Ramos, Torreón, and Magistral. The productive Real de Oro de Agua Caliente mine was also in danger. In the month of May alone, Indian renegades killed more than a hundred vecinos. Many Spanish residents abandoned their outlying ranches, and several silver mines curtailed production because of the impossibility of safe transportation of supplies and ore.[25]

After only a short rest from his six-month expedition, O'Conor set out to reprimand the Tarahumara rebels. On June 11, 1732, he rode south with 125 officers and men of the First Compañía Volante, leaving the other three companies under Captain Manuel Múñoz to protect Chihuahua and Captain Domingo Díaz to guard against hit-and-run raids from out of the Bolsón. O'Conor's display of force produced little; he found no renegades and participated in no battles. On June 14, he arrived at the Tarahumara mission of San Pablo, met with the Indian governor, received assurances the Indians would remain faithful to the king, and confiscated their bows and arrows. On June 18, he encountered seventeen Indian laborers returning to their village from a recent hacienda harvest. Supposing them potential troublemakers, he seized their weapons, sent them on their way, and retired to the hacienda of Atotonico. There he received news of a large force of renegade warriors camped at the south end of the Bolsón.[26]

To prevent further hostilities in the south, O'Conor dispatched 125 troops of the First Compañía Volante and 50 regular dragoons to serve temporarily in seven places from Santa Rita, Los Patos, and Santo Domingo as far as El Gallo. By covering the entire territory from Ancón de Carros to the Río Nazas, he hoped to keep Indian renegades in check. Yet from the sierras of Chivato and Carrizo, Tarahumara laborers arrived to work the valley's harvest, and to avoid any mistakes by his troops or retaliation from edgy vecinos, O'Conor asked the local Spanish official in charge of the Indian district to delay a recent order sending Tarahumaras to labor in the interior and to prohibit them from traveling about armed.[27]

In the northeast, nomadic Mescaleros and Lipánes completely rejected the disciplined life of the religious mission which offered little they needed or wanted. As such problems increased, O'Conor reevaluated his tactics, already losing validity due to the Tarahumara renegades. On July 26, he reported to the viceroy that Tarahumaras supposedly congregated in mission villages quite often left, turning to highway robbery to maintain themselves. "One never knows," predicted O'Conor, "when they will be at peace or at war."[28] He proposed that estate owners and missionaries coordinate their efforts to keep the Tarahumaras in check. If ranchers wanted labor and missionaries sought Christian souls, both needed to replace past antagonism with cooperation. O'Conor further urged daily roll calls and issuance of special licenses for travel between mission and landed estate.[29]

In November of 1773, O'Conor led a column of troops northward into the rugged recesses of the Sierra Guadalupe and Sierra Organos against Mescalero and Natagée Apaches. He maneuvered a band of Indians into two fights, killed some forty-five warriors, and destroyed several rancherías. The rest scattered, and O'Conor's forces, fully exhausted, turned back in search of badly needed supplies. His success removed some of the friction between army and citizenry, but murder and property loss in Coahuila, Sonora, and Nueva Vizcaya continued. As a consequence, O'Conor turned to a policy of pointedly distributing gifts through his frontier line officers, relying less on the mission fathers to implement the program of gift-giving.[30]

Two years later, Commandant Inspector O'Conor concluded his frontier inspection and reorganized presidio defenses to meet the fixed-post requirements of the Reglamento. Though he negotiated an alliance in Coahuila with Lipán chieftains Javierillo and Cabello Largo, he failed to break the Apache-Tarahumara alliance in Nueva Vizcaya. On September 23, 1775, O'Conor launched his first general campaign against this northern alliance. Deploying his own 340 troops plus militiamen from Sonora, Texas, and New Mexico, he hoped to defeat the rebels by using converging columns. Though the campaigners supposedly killed 130 enemy warriors and took 104 prisoners, the three-month effort failed to rid the interior provinces of these particular Indian rebels.[31]

In September of 1776, the commandant inspector mounted a second major offensive against the Eastern Apaches, accomplishing little more than keeping his command supplied during a two-month futile march from one sierra to another. Five skirmishes with the Indians netted twenty-six dead and eighteen captured. O'Conor reached El Paso in early November, but a serious illness forced him to turn the expedition over to Lieutenant Colonel Francisco Bellido of San Eleazario. Attempting to duplicate the success of 1775, Bellido split his command, but managed to kill only forty rebels, take forty-six prisoner (mostly women and children), and recover 119 horses and mules. Finally, "the grave illness from which I suffer," declared O'Conor, forced transferral of the commandancy to Lieutenant Colonel Manuel Múñoz. With Viceroy Bucareli's permission, O'Conor then returned to Mexico City.[32]

On July 22, 1777, the retired O'Conor filed his general assessment of frontier conditions. In it, he assured his replacement that the chain of frontier forts had enough equipment and provisions to deal with Indian hostiles, but before leaving for Yucatán to assume its governorship, he displayed skepticism. Writing to José de Gálvez, now minister of the Indies, he expressed doubts about the effectiveness of fixed-post defenses, peacemaking policy, and commented that he left the frontier with a great sense of relief.[33] Thus, after some initial success, centered around protecting the frontier's mining and ranching interest, he constructed a chain of frontier defenses. Considering his resources, it is a wonder he helped remove a major obstacle to frontier development. Though he aligned and garrisoned the fixed-posts and mounted major campaigns against Indian renegades, he failed to eliminate the unconquered Indian strongholds of northern New Spain. Nor did he break cultural and political contact between separated northern kinsmen. Even for the great number of Indians who were in missions, the Indian strongholds were an ever-present option during the latter part of the eighteenth century. They, as much as anything, forced Spain to modify its northern Indian policy.

CHAPTER VI

FOOTNOTES

[1] See Lafora, Relación del viaje; Moorhead, The Presidio, 56-57; and John, Storms Brewed in Other Men's Worlds, 431-64.

[2] Rubí, Digttamen que de orden del Exmo. Señor Marqués de Croix, Virrey de este Reyno, expone el Mariscal de Campo Marqués de Rubí, en orden a la mejor situación de los Presidios para la defensa y extensión de su Frontera a la Gentilidad en los Confines al Norte de este Virreynatto, Tacubaya, April 10, 1768, AGI, Guadalajara 511.

[3] Reglamento de 1772, previously cited, and its English translation: Sidney B. Brinckerhoff and Odie B. Faulk, Lancers for the King: A Study of the Frontier Military System of Northern New Spain, with a Translation of the Royal Regulations of 1772.

[4] See for example, Donald Winslow Rowland, "The Elizondo Expedition Against the Indian Rebels of Sonora, 1765-1771," unpublished Ph.D. dissertation, University of California, Berkeley, 1930.

[5] Colonel Domingo Elizondo to Viceroy Marqués de Croix, Pitic, November 5, 1769, AGI Guadalajara 416. For the "plano del corazon de Cerro Prieto," see Mario Hernández Sánchez-Barba, La última expansión española en America, 232.

[6] Viceroy Croix to Minister of the Indies Arriaga, Mexico, April 25, May 26, and June 27, 1769 (enclosed with Extractos de Novedades), AGI, Guadalajara 416 and AGI, Mexico 2429.

[7] Gálvez to Croix, Santa Cruz de Mayo, May 14, 1769, AGI, Guadalajara 416; Gálvez to Ministro de la Guerra, Gregorio Muniain, Santa Cruz de Mayo, May 12, 1769, AGI, Mexico 2429.

[8] Elizondo to Croix, Pitic, November 5, 1769, AGI, Guadalajara 416 and AGI, Mexico 1369.

[9] For example, on June 10, 1769, Gálvez proposed that Mayo, Pima, and Yaqui leaders be organized into eight companies of Indian auxiliaries, to be called compañías de indios nobles; they would be exempt from paying tribute, receive double allotments of suertes (land parcels), and be allowed to use Spanish weapons. The experiment was never implemented. Gálvez to Croix, No. 13, Alamos, June 10, 1769, AGI, Guadalajara 416.

[10] Frey Antonio Canales and Frey Antonio María de los Reyes to José de Fayni, Durango, September 4, 1771, AGI, Guadalajara 512; Royal Order of August 10, 1769, AGI, Indiferente General 1713; On Viceroy Bucareli, See Rómulo Velasco Ceballos, ed., La Administracion de D.Frey Antonio María de Bucareli y Ursúa, Cuadragesima sexto virrey de Mexico, 2 vols.; A middle-of-the-road account is provided in Bernard E. Bobbs, The Viceregency of Antonio María Bucareli in New Spain, 1771-1779.

[11]The exceptionally competent O'Conor served in Cuba (1763-65) under his first cousin the Mariscal de Campo Alejandro O' Reilly. Transferred to Mexico, he served on General Juan de Villalba's staff and also as a special inspector to Texas. He was provisional governor of Texas from 1767 to 1770, commandant of the garrison at San Fernando de Austria in Coahuila from 1770 to 1771, military commandant in Nueva Vizcaya from 1771 to 1772, then commandant inspector of the northern provinces by appointment of September 14, 1772. See David M. Vigness, "Don Hugo O'Conor and New Spain's Northeastern Frontier, 1764-1776," Journal of the West 6 (January 1967): 28-35.

[12]Governor José de Fayni to Arriaga, Mexico, December 27, 1771, AGI, Guadalajara 512; Fayni to Bucareli, Durango, February 28, 1772 (enclosed with Bucareli to Arriaga, No. 295, Mexico, March 18, 1772), AGI, Guadalajara 513.

[13]Lieutenant Antonio Felix Sánchez to Governor Antonio de Mendoza, No. 1, Buenaventura, April 29, 1775, AGI, Guadalajara 194.

[14]O'Conor relinquished command in January of 1777, leaving, besides the twenty-two presidial companies, four roving companies in Nueva Vizcaya, one in Sonora, and two detachments of regular dragoons commanded by 6 captains and totaling 623 soldiers and 120 Indian scouts--their salaries amounting to 162,581 pesos a year. Also maintained were 3,396 horses and mules. The total military forces had 2,311 officers and men (including militiamen and Indian scouts), and the total expense to the royal treasury was 616,761 pesos a year. Moorhead, The Presidio, 72-73.

[15]O'Conor to Bucareli, Diario de operaciones, Chihuahua, February 18, 1772 (enclosed with Bucareli to Arriaga, Nos. 2 and 3, Mexico, April 24, 1772) in Velasco Ceballos, La administración de D. Frey Antonio María de Bucareli, 1: 38-41.

[16]Fayni to Bucareli, Chihuahua, February 1, 1772 (enclosed with Bucareli to Arriaga, April 24, 1772) in Velasco Ceballos, La administración de D. Antonio María de Bucareli, 1: 35-38.

[17]Bucareli to Arriaga, Mexico, April 24, 1772, in Velasco Ceballos, La administración de D. Antonio María de Bucareli, 1: 41-43.

[18]Bucareli to Arriaga, No. 451, Mexico, June 26, 1772 (enclosed with Extracto de Noticias de las Provincias Internas), AGN, Correspondencia de los virreyes, Bucareli, Tomo 25.

[19]Barón de Riperdá to Bucareli, Béjar, November 28, 1772 and December 3, 1772, AGI, Guadalajara 513; Bucareli to Riperdá, Mexico, January 6, 1773, AGI, Guadalajara 513.

[20]Bucareli to Arriaga, No. 1524, Mexico, September 26, 1774. In Velasco Ceballos, La administración de D. Frey Antonio María de Bucareli, 1: 178-81. On the Navajo, see Frank Reeve, "Navajo-Spanish Diplomacy, 1770-1790," NMHR 35 (July 1960): 200-35.

21Thomas, The Plains Indians and New Mexico, 177-83.

22Bucareli, Extracto de Novedades, Mexico, January 27, 1773 (enclosed with Bucareli to Arriaga, No. 733 Mexico, same place and date), AGI, Guadalajara 513.

23Bucareli, Extracto de Novedades, Mexico, January 27, 1773 (enclosed with Bucareli to Arriaga, No. 1014, Mexico, same place and date), AGI, Guadalajara 514.

24O'Conor to Bucareli, San Fernando de Austria, March 31, 1773 (enclosed with Bucareli to Arriaga, Mexico, April 26, 1773), AGI, Guadalajara 513.

25Captain Manuel de Villaverde to Ayudante Mayor Juan de San Vicente, Hacienda de la Mimbrera, June 7, 1773; Captain Domingo Díaz to San Vicente, San Bartolomé, June 8, 1773, AGI Guadalajara 514.

26O'Conor Diario de operaciones, Atotonilco, June 23, 1773, AGI, Guadalajara 514. See also Navarro García, Don José de Gálvez, 229-31.

27O'Conor to Bucareli, Cerro Gordo, July 3, 1773 (enclosed with Diario de operaciones, June 24-July 3, 1773); Bucareli, Extracto de Novedades, Mexico, July 27, 1773 (enclosed with Bucareli to Arriaga, No. 1014, Mexico, same place and date), AGI, Guadalajara 514.

28O'Conor to Bucareli, Chihuahua, July 26, 1773 (enclosed with Extracto de Novedades), AGI, Guadalajara 514.

29Ibid.

30O'Conor, Diario de operaciones, Junta de los Ríos, November 18, and December, 1773, AGI Guadalajara 513; O'Conor Informe sobre la provincia de Sonora y Nueva Vizcaya, August 14, 1774-April 19, 1776 AGN, PI, 88 (f. 27-139).

31O'Conor to Bucareli, Carrizal, December 1, 1775 (enclosed with Bucareli to Arriaga, No. 2108, Mexico, January 27, 1776), AGI, Guadalajara 515.

32Bucareli to Gálvez, no. 2706, Mexico, January 27, 1777 (enclosed with Extracto de Novedades, same place and date), AGI, Guadalajara 515.

33Hugo O'Conor died in Mérida, Yucatán on March 8, 1779. O'Conor, Estado . . . de Presidios, Mexico, July 22, 1777 (enclosed with O'Conor to Gálvez, Mexico, July 27, 1777), AGI, Guadalajara 516. For publication of this document, see Enrique Gonzalez Flores and Francisco R. Almada, eds., Informe de Hugo O'Conor sobre el estado de las Provincias Internas del Norte, 1771-1776. Also see Mary Lu Moore and Delmar L. Beene, eds., "The Interior Provinces of New Spain: The Report of Hugo O'Conor, January 20, 1776," Arizona and the West 13 (1971): 265-82.

CHAPTER VII

CREATION OF THE COMMANDANCY GENERAL
AND THE YUMA BID FOR FREEDOM,
1776-1782

It was 1776. Adam Smith published his classical politico-economic treaties, Wealth of Nations. Great Britain's intransigent American colonies continued to assemble in Philadelphia. And Bourbon authorities, reevaluating Spain's position and goals in the far northern provinces, contemplated an important political change there. Recently, Commandant Inspector Hugo O'Conor's military command indicated the value of combining the northern provinces, an idea earlier favored by Don José de Gálvez. Now back in Spain, Gálvez convinced the king to create an officially recognized separate northern command. And in this auspicious year-- 1776--Charles III authorized a distinct administrative unit in New Spain, comprised of the joined Provincias Internas del Norte. He appointed as commandant general a highly capable officer, quick of mind, articulate, and fiercely loyal to the king--the Caballero Teodoro de Croix.[1]

Charles's instructions to Croix allowed him almost viceregal powers. The commandant inspector, as well as the six northern governors, from Texas to California, would all answer to the commandant general who in turn was to communicate directly with His Majesty through Minister of the Indies Gálvez. Sharing authority with Viceroy Bucareli in the new province of Upper California, Croix would additionally serve as general superintendent of the treasury and vice patron of the Church in the Provincias Internas. The main objective of the independent frontier command was defense against the Indians, but the king's instructions as usual suggested an enlightened goal--"conversion of the numerous nations of heathen Indians who live in the north of western America." Commandant General Croix was to unify frontier forces by "reinvigorating" presidio defenses and local militia in the strict accord with the Reglamento of 1772, establish new defensive towns, and pacify the numerous tribes hostile to Christianity by "good treatment" as required by the Recopilación de leyes de los reynos de las Indias. Croix's orders also entailed amnesty and placatory gifts to Indian rebels as a continued feature of frontier policy.[2]

On January 21, 1777, Teodoro de Croix entered Mexico City and presented himself to Viceroy Bucareli. A petty rift soon developed between the two since Bucareli felt insulted at having to share authority in the northern provinces. Also, Bucareli trusted in O'Conor's administration and Croix's criticism of both it and the viceroy's ideas for special integration of the Indians angered him. The commandant general spent seven months in the capital, conferring with Bucareli and organizing his official staff. He chose Lieutenant Colonel José Rubio to replace the retired O'Conor, appointed Captain Antonio de Bonilla (previously adjutant inspector under O'Conor) to the new office of secretary of the commandancy, and selected

Pedro Galindo Navarro, a lawyer, as his auditor of war. He also appointed Father Juan Agustín Morfi, well-qualified by broad experience and travels, to serve as his chaplain.[3]

Before leaving Mexico City on August 4, 1777, Croix received disconcerting news from the frontier provinces. From Sonora, Governor Juan Bautista de Anza reported renewed Seri and Pima uprisings as well as desertion by Seris imprisoned at Pitic. From Nueva Vizcaya, Captain Domingo Díaz of the First Compañía Volante informed Croix that 200 Apache warriors, operating from eight rancherías within the Bolsón de Mapimí, had ransacked the estate of San Juan Bautista de Casta and the ranches of La Cueva and Patrón. In retaliation, Díaz had maneuvered an Indian band into two fights near the Bolsón, killed two major chieftains (Calvo and Conejo), destroyed their rancherías, and recovered considerable booty, including the banner of the San Saba mission in Texas. Nueva Vizcaya's Governor Felipe Barri wrote further that Tarahumara rebels dressed as vaqueros had attacked the Real de Mapimí, stealing the mules and leaving the mines inoperative and that south of the Bolsón, some 300 warriors killed 76 people and took more than 1,000 head of cattle, sheep, and goats during raids on haciendas and ranches near San Miguel de Aguayo.[4]

In route to his new command, Croix was swamped with more bad news. Sonora reported growing unrest among the normally peaceful Opatas; Yaquis and Mayos were again abandoning their mission villages; Seris were joining Gileños and Piato kinsmen around the Cerro Prieto; and Seri leader Boquinete reportedly was organizing a war party to liberate the remaining Seris held at Pitic. Nueva Vizcaya was under siege by Apache raiders around San Buenaventura, El Paso, Babonyaba, and Chihuahua. Tarahumara renegades joined them in harassing frontier settlements. Supposedly at peace, Lipán Apaches in Coahuila raided poblador communities, attributing the forays to Mescaleros. In Texas, the Comanches and Nations of the North increased their ambushes, and Lipánes raided south as far as San Antonio while Comanches, Utes, Navajos, and Apaches continued to devastate New Mexico.[5]

Preoccupied with the desperate need to secure the more interior provinces, Croix nonetheless was drawn into the continual bickering between missionary and temporal officials concerning the methods of Indian secularization. In Sonora, Sinaloa, Nueva Vizcaya, and Coahuila, Bourbon officials and mission fathers continually bickered over the efforts of pacifying the hostile tribes, but in some provinces, an unprecedented success at spreading the "faith" caused vociferous defense of missionary rights when confronted with military interference. In the early 1770s, military officials in California, frustrated by Indian banditry and hit-and-run raids near the settlements, attempted to prevent pacification welfarism among mission Indians, insisting that the gift-giving not only included food and clothing, but weapons. Franciscan fathers resentful of this interference, accused presidio commanders of inciting rebellion and, in turn, the military charged the missionaries with fomenting sedition. Croix, too far removed geographically and concerned with the fixed-post defenses, could do little but encourage his military administrators to practice some patience with the mission fathers.[6]

Even as the new commandancy formed, Indian unrest demanded attention. The reality of sedition and open rebellion absorbed Croix's time and energy, forcing temporary abandonment of other Bourbon objectives. Governor de Anza suppressed the Seri uprising of 1777, but Seri leader Boquinete and a handful of followers allied with Gila River Apaches continued attacking and ambushing in Sonora. In frustration, Croix recommended the Seris be rounded up and sent overseas. But the king refused to approve such a request, and late in 1779, the Seris revolted again. Gálvez's visions of northwestern economic expansion were set aside as Croix and his successors, attempted to provide strategic defense by readjusting the chain of frontier forts, founding defensive towns, and seeking to pacify Indian people.[7]

Teodoro de Croix convened three war councils during his four-year tenure. The third and most significant council, held at Chihuahua in the summer of 1778, included former governor of New Mexico, Pedro Fermín de Mendinueta; Mendinueta's replacement, Juan Bautista de Anza; the governor of Nueva Vizcaya; and various influential citizens of the provinces. Though not forgetful of Bourbon desires for economic development, centered around mining and predicated on access to native labor, Croix formulated Indian policy on the first-hand experience of local frontier captains and the reality of the frontier and its Indian cultures. His frontline officers, for example, recommended the enlistment of the Nations of the North as allies for warfare against the Apaches, a policy of pitting Eastern Apache groups against one another, and substantial enlargement of presidial forces staffed by mixed bloods and Indians.[8] Successful assembly and equipping of a truly effective Indian-fighting force, with adequate resources, had been tried in the past, but Croix had a real chance to demonstrate the possibilities of its success.

Verging on war with England, Spain fixed a restrictive timetable for Croix's Indian policy. On July 23, 1779, he received royal instructions to abandon plans for a major offensive, keeping any actions nonmilitary, and to pacify Indian people through gift-giving. Presumably, the Indians would slowly come to prefer European goods to their own and Croix could urge their use of firearms for hunting and defense. Thus, introducing such commodities and firearms to unconquered tribes, the Bourbons hoped to create Indian dependency on frontier society which would encourage their becoming productive frontier citizens. But the 1779 Royal Order merely frustrated Croix's plan for a general offensive campaign.[9]

The possible opening of an overland supply route from Sonora to California also caused problems. On January 6, 1774, Captain Juan Bautista de Anza, of the Pimería Alta presidio of Tubac, set out to survey a possible land route from his small garrison to the coastal settlement of San Diego. Passing through Yuma country at the junction of the Gila and Colorado rivers, his party received the friendly hospitality of Yuma leader Olleyquotequiebe, christened Salvador Palma by the Franciscans. On May 26, Anza returned to Tubac, having covered some 769 leagues (about 2,000 miles).[10]

In June of 1774, Viceroy Bucareli, openly pleased with the results of the Anza expedition, ordered Governor Francisco Antonio Crespo of Sonora to find Palma and establish friendly relations with him through gifts, food rations, and other inducements to render him dependent on Spanish society. Anza implemented the tried and practiced program of buying off Indians and reported in November of 1774 that five or six Yuma rancherías had accepted the gifts and requested more rations and gifts. Therefore, by November's end, Captain Anza was in the capital, helping plan another expedition.[11]

The next year, newly promoted Lieutenant Colonel Anza and 240 colonists left Horcasitas, Sonora for Monterey, California on a second expedition. In Yuma territory the expeditionary force again enjoyed Salvador Palma's cordial welcome. The negotiations went smoothly, and before helping the colonists across the river, Palma asked Fray Francisco Garcés to begin Christian work among his people.[12]

In early January, 1776, the expedition arrived at Mission San Gabriel in southern California. Anza and the commanding officer in California, Captain Fernando de Rivera y Moncada, immediately marched south to help suppress an Indian revolt in San Diego. They subdued the Diegueño rebels and Rivera, fearing further Indian unrest, delayed Anza three weeks in San Diego. As Rivera took no decisive action, the lieutenant colonel proceeded independently to San Gabriel. With a small force, he then went on to San Francisco Bay where he selected sites for the presidio of San Francisco, a mission nearby on the Arroyo de Dolores, and the pueblo of San José.[13]

On completion of his extensive expedition, Anza proposed for the Yumas a modified form of mission life. He knew and liked them well and believed them unwilling to submit to the rigorous requirements of a religious mission. Yet Anza did not disregard the military needs of the California project. In fact, he strongly urged creation of two garrisons on the Colorado and Gila rivers. On the other hand, Father Garcés saw the Yuma project as an expansion of mission autonomy and suggested eventual establishment of fifteen missions among the Octams, Cocomaricopas, Mohaves, and other northwestern nations, using Yuma villages as operational bases.[14]

On November 20, 1776, Lieutenant Colonel Anza warned Viceroy Bucareli that they must exercise great care in winning over the Yumas. Anza also cautioned against any interference with the fragile Yuma economy.[15] Despite the fertility of the Gila River Valley, the Yumas' streamway farming techniques produced just enough to support themselves, and vecinos moving there would have to provision themselves to last through their own first harvest. Equally important, Anza demanded discipline among the settlers and reasonable relations between religious and temporal officials to avoid conflicts leading to other Indian rebellions.[16]

Ignoring the handwriting on the wall, Commandant General Croix proceeded with his plans to construct a military colony in Yuma country to protect the California supply road. Croix originally wanted a presidio at the confluence of the Gila and Colorado, drawing troops from the garrisons of Horcasitas and Buenavista, but possible hostile actions by rebellious Seris, Gileños, and Upper Pimas required keeping those presidios at full strength. His funding also restricted, Croix decided to place a twenty-two man presidial force at the strategic position to protect the mission and Spanish settlement destined for Yuma country.

Besides, had not the prominent Yuma leader Salvador Palma requested missionaries? Palma, his brother Ignacio, the son of Captain Pablo, and one other Indian had even accompanied Anza to Mexico City in 1776; Anza served as godfather to Palma when he received baptism into the Christian faith during an elaborate ceremony in the cathedral. Viceroy Bucareli thought "the 664 peso cost to the viceroyalty was well worth it, in order to secure a lasting peace, for these Indians are the ones who can open or close the passage between Sonora, New Mexico, and California."17 The Spaniards even encouraged Palma to stay in Mexico City until early 1777, entertaining and indoctrinating him and hoping for his aid in achieving Bourbon goals on the Colorado. In November, Palma presented to the viceroy a memorial stressing a need for mission work among his people, and listing Indian nations possibly susceptible to his influence if the viceroy wanted allies. He named Jalchedunes, Jamajáes, Pimas, Opatas, Cocomaricopas, Cajuenes, Jaliquamas, Cucupas, Comeías, Pápagos, and the Apaches who lived on the opposite bank of the Colorado.18 Seemingly sincere in his request, Palma also understood the advantages of an alliance in the pacification of neighboring tribes. He declared, "the only self interest which might induce me would be the desire to acquire Spanish arms to defend myself against my enemies, as I learn other nations have done."19

In some respects, Anza's success among the Yumas worked against him. He completely won over Salvador Palma, and viceroyal officials, ignoring Anza's earlier warnings, took for granted an easy success on the Colorado. Full realization of economic development and spiritual ventures required both linkage of New Mexico with Sonora and California and solution of New Mexico's Comanche problems. Anza's renown as an explorer and excellent record as a soldier and diplomat made him the obvious choice for the job in New Mexico, and sometime in 1776, Viceroy Bucareli proposed him as governor of New Mexico. Croix wanted Anza as governor in Sonora where he could continue directing the Yuma experiment, but in May of 1777, Spain appointed Anza to serve in New Mexico.20

Salvador Palma returned from his dazzling Mexico City reception with a new suit of clothing, a cane of authority, and the viceroy's promises of missionaries, a protective presidio, and many gifts. Bucareli also gave him a military title and assurances of viceregal support at the confluence of the Colorado and Gila Rivers. Indeed, the attention accorded him increased Palma's stature and influence among his immediate followers. But when the promises failed to materialize and his people started to ridicule him, Palma visited the presidio of Altar, desperately pleading to Captain Pedro de Tueros for the overdue gifts, military allies, and missionaries.21

Palma had no way of knowing that Teodoro de Croix, preoccupied with rebellious Seris, had postponed royal orders of February 10 and 14, 1777, approving missionaries and a military colony among the Yumas. Increasing raids in central Sonora by Upper Pimas and Gileños, rumors of an Opata revolt, plus a serious illness put Croix's military reorganization behind schedule and further contributed to his anxiety. On February 5, 1779, at the urgent request of Captain Tueros, the commandant general made an indecisive effort from his sickbed in Chihuahua. Until he could take personal command, he wanted Fathers Garcés and Juan Díaz to visit Palma and reassure him of forthcoming gifts and mission fathers.22

But Father Garcés attempted to work around the commandant general. Remembering Viceroy Bucareli's reputation for pious works and his personal interest in the land route to California, Garcés wrote directly to him on March 11, 1779, asking assistance in purchasing gifts for the Yumas. But before his letter reached the capital, Bucareli died, and the executors of his estate refused the petition. After months of delay, the fathers and a small military escort crossed the desert in mid-August. Díaz turned back, and though Garcés reached Palma's village, his meager gifts of tobacco, sugar, cloth, and glass beads satisfied no one. Also, Palma seemed unable to control his following, and the arrival of Díaz with ten more soldiers early in October merely added more mouths and promises, both empty.[23]

From the new mission of La Purísima Concepción del Río Colorado, Díaz wrote Croix of his difficulty in stopping intertribal warfare on the Colorado, adding that Palma's brother Ignacio was inciting sedition among young Yuma warriors. Father Díaz doubted their ability to rise in full rebellion but suggested that Ignacio Palma be closely watched or removed from the area. Croix immediately instructed the young commander of the new military settlement, Ensign Santiago de Islas, to make surveillance of Ignacio a top priority and to report at once any signs of sedition.[24]

Ignacio's emergence as a significant leader proved critical for Salvador Palma. Though Salvador convinced his followers to refrain from their customary profitable wars with neighboring tribes by promises of an alliance and gifts, the viceroyalties long delay and token efforts of Fray Díaz undermined his leadership. His influence waned so much that Father Díaz feared Ignacio's faction would conspire to murder Salvador. Discretion required extreme caution for the slightest carelessness could cause a major uprising.[25]

The settlement plan finally adopted after months of heated debate was an impractical compromise between the Order of Franciscan fathers and Commandant General Croix. The Franciscans, stripped of all but spiritual control, were to instruct, baptize, and encourage the Yumas to join the settlement. Croix temporarily assigned temporal authority to Ensign Islas, empowering him to administer in accordance with pertinent articles of the Reglamento of 1772, the Recopilación de leyes de los reynos de las Indias, and such additional orders as Croix himself might issue.[26]

Government of the proposed colony would be exclusively military with defense shared by soldiers and vecinos. Yumas voluntarily joining the colony would be incorporated into resident colonists but with accompanying obligations. Specifically, to be declared legal vecinos, Indians would cultivate their assigned land parcels and take their turn at maintaining public buildings and utilities. Each Indian resident would share in cultivating the settlement's revenue-producing land, thus being obliged to support the garrison both militarily and economically.[27]

Yumas were to undergo no forcible conscription, either as militia units or laborers, nor were they to suffer any discrimination in the allotment of land. On the contrary, Croix's military assessor, Pedro Galindo Navarro, suggested that existing Yuman rancherías be left undisturbed until the commandant could better understand their land-use patterns. But these particular plans do not soundly evidence equal treatment of the Yumas; they merely indicate secular intentions. As with previous royal policy and regulations, actual enforcement of instructions diminished in direct proportion to geographical distance from central authority.[28]

The first vecinos, mostly mixed blood soldiers' families, arrived in late December of 1780. Each received a subsidy of ten pesos a month for the first year, a yoke of oxen, two cows, one bull, two mares and construction tools. Lands and water rights were distributed equally among soldiers, settlers, and those few Yumas voluntarily joining the colony. The best lands went for the town commons, building began, and work seemed to go smoothly, but Croix's desire for two small towns of twenty-five families each, built amidst three thousand agitated Yumas, required a small miracle.[29]

By January of 1781, two small pueblos existed on the west bank of the Colorado--Purísma Concepción, near the Gila junction, and San Pedro y San Pablo de Bicuñer, some five leagues (about thirteen miles) upstream. Two more missionaries, Juan Antonio Joaquín de Barreneche and Joseph Matías Moreno, joined Garcés and Díaz as companions. Yumas knew the intruders as rather strange visitors inclined toward generous gift-giving, but this new circumstance of Spanish residents settling nearby shocked them, and as food rations ran low, tension mounted.[30]

Salvador Palma fully understood the expediency of easing the tension for Spanish allies could serve his established plan, but he could not allow them superiority since Yuma factionalism as well as discord among the vecinos complicated the situation.

The Colorado colonization effort moved along for another six months, but everything conspired against its success. Supplies constantly lacked, land yielded little, and the outsiders' livestock ate and trampled Yuma crops. As expected the gifts and rations of food failed to arrive, Yumas tired of supplying their own food to the vecinos and became more unruly. Also interfering in their lives, Ensign Islas appointed Salvador Palma governor of Concepción, named his brother Ignacio governor of Bicuñer, and designated Yuma leader Pablo fiscal de la iglesia (church leader) of Bicuñer. He then used these Indian officials to punish Yuma troublemakers. But in early June, Islas arrested Ignacio and Pablo, accusing them of conspiring to murder a soldier. This further embittered Yuma leaders whose growing anger over Ensign Islas's continued encroachments fueled a determination to compromise no longer.[31] Finally, Captain Fernando de Rivera arrived with a California-bound contingent of Spaniards, livestock, and supplies. Sending the others on ahead, Rivera fattened livestock on Yuma lands.

Irate, Yuma leaders called a war council, allied the various factions and on Tuesday, July 17, 1781, the Yumas rebelled. They killed the four missionaries, all soldiers and male settlers except seven, whom they held captive with seventy-five women and children. At the Concepción mission, perhaps because Garcés was celebrating mass, they at first spared him and his companion Barreneche, but warriors surrounded Islas and his detachment and killed them outright. At Bicuñer, Fathers Díaz and Matías died in the initial onslaught. The next day other warriors moved against the crude barricade hastily constructed by Captain Rivera and his eleven soldiers. After a short battle, defenses collapsed and the soldiers were killed. Salvador Palma wanted to spare Father Garcés, but his brother disagreed and on Thursday, July 19, 1781, the Yumas sought out and killed Garcés and Barreneche.[32]

The Yumas killed or ate most of the livestock and divided horses and other war booty among their leaders. They gathered captured women and children in a central location, without desire to harm them, they proceeded to completely devastate the two towns. Yuma leaders also directed total destruction of the two mission churches, together with the images, records, and furnishings to wipe out every vestige of Spanish influence on the Colorado and Gila rivers.[33]

Learning of the disaster, Commandant General Croix summoned Anza's replacement in Sonora, Governor Jacobo Ugarte y Loyola, and other officers to a war council at Arizpe.[34] At its recommendation, Croix ordered Lieutenant Colonel Pedro Fages of the Compañía Franca de Voluntarios de Cataluña (The Free Company of Catalonian Volunteers) to the Colorado River with a hastily organized expedition. If met peaceably by the Yumas, Fages would seize only the two Palmas and their lieutenants, but if they continued fighting, he was to show no mercy. Croix ordered the troops to ransom the captives safely, then retrieve all items given and take all booty possible since the only object of the negotiations was return of the prisoners. Fages failed to defeat the Yumas or even capture the rebel leaders, but he did negotiate and ransomed the seventy-four captives for tobacco and other goods.[35]

In the summer of 1782, when the joint Sonora-California expedition under Fages and California governor Felipe de Neve brought no victory over the Yumas, Croix decided to take no further action against them. He now deemed a Spanish settlement on the Colorado impractical and unnecessary since needed supplies or remounts could be forced through to California by an expedition. "In truth," wrote Croix, "the Yumas are no more treacherous, inconsistent, stubborn, and wild, than any other Indians on this frontier."[36] Avoiding them presented no difficulty. A war council at Arizpe in January of 1783 declared the banks of the Colorado and Gila rivers unsuitable for maintaining a Spanish settlement and recommended abandonment of further efforts to garrison the junction.[37]

Vulnerable to embarrassing charges of undue delay and inadequate support of the Yuma colony, Croix attributed the revolt to "the unfortunate representations" made by Juan Bautista de Anza and Father Garcés.[38] Indeed, Anza and Garcés had exaggerated both the tribal power and responsibility of Salvador Palma and the productivity of Yuma lands. Anza warned earlier of calamitous results of attempting a settlement without a strong garrison, advising adequate provisioning of vecinos to avoid straining the Yuma economy, and urging respect of Indian rights, but he remained Croix's prime scapegoat. Though Anza negotiated an unprecedented Comanche peace in New Mexico and had strong support from the new commandant general, Jacobo Ugarte, and Commandant Inspector José Antonio Rengel, he eventually lost the governorship of Sonora.[39]

Croix's inability to provide adequate military protection for the vecinos and Ensign Islas's failure to establish satisfactory relations with the Yumas led to the revolt. Croix, obviously disappointed by the failure of his commanding officer to keep him adequately informed of the situation, asserted that from the very beginning, Islas believed his troops sufficient to humble the Indians should problems arise. This grave misjudgment and Croix's opinions based on Islas's exaggerated reports, coupled with the unity and strength of the Yumas, foretold rebellion. Yet Croix adamantly blamed the Yuma Revolt on misrepresentation by Anza and Garcés.[40]

Though aware that Teodoro de Croix labored under the burden of economic reorganization with overwhelming problems and responsibilities, the missionaries never forgave him for blaming the martyred Garcés. They derided his proposed colony on the Colorado as an effort against the proper missions and presidios proposed by Viceroy Bucareli. The fathers always remembered the disaster 1781, and their disenchantment with Bourbon development of the Provincias Internas lasted until the end of the colonial period. They battled forcibly with some of Croix's successors, particularly Pedro de Nava, and continually requested return of viceregal jurisdiction over Pimería Alta, believing Bucareli best represented their proselytizing interests. The Bourbon Crown continued to ignore their pleas.[41]

Similar to other frontier revolts, the Yuma conspiracy involved a marginal leadership. Rebels besides the two Palmas included Pablo, son of important Yuma leader Captain Pablo, and two Indian interpreters, Joseph and Francisco Xavier. Joseph, from Concepción, and Francisco, from Bicuñer, provided valuable background information on the settlements' strengths and weaknesses. Though two released prisoners testified that Francisco Xavier, Ignacio Palma, and Pablo actually led the uprising, the evidence indicates that Salvador reached accord with his brother and played the major role in the revolt. Lieutenants Ignacio and Pablo represented the limit of Salvador's direct influence on tribal action, but under his persuasive directions, they, Francisco Xavier, and Joseph mobilized the Yuma people from most of the surrounding rancherías to rise up in successful rebellion.

The Yuma Revolt is comparable in violence and bloodshed to Tepehuán and Pueblo hostility but differs from them in important ways. The Yumas never were reconquered, and in contrast to the falling out between Popé and his lieutenants, the coherence of Yuma organizers seemed to strengthen considerably as the revolt progressed. The two Palmas, especially, gained in personal status and tribal control after proving their organizational talents. No northern conspiracy like that of the Tepehuán and Tarahumara followed the Yuma uprising, but Lieutenant Colonel Fages's failure to subdue, humble, or even capture Yuma leaders testifies to their strength--both individually and as a tribe.

Similarities between the Tepehúan, Yuman, Tarahumara, and Yaqui rebellions include unencompassing missionary influence, unthwarted Indian religious practices, and obviously vacillating methods of secular influence. As in the Seri Revolt, Yuma hostility derived from Spanish colonial usurpation of land and disrespect of Indian water rights. The crucial question, division, restriction, and assignment of land parcels created the tension leading to the conspiracy.

Assessment of the leadership roles contributes significantly to an understanding of the various revolts. Both Luis Oacpicagigua of the Upper Pimas and Salvador Palma of the Yumas held considerable influence among their people, and military officials, with good reason, respected their oratorical abilities and the esteem accorded them. But Luis lacked strong tribal following since many Pima leaders, already steeped in frontier society, refused to sacrifice its benefits in a revolt. In Palma's case, the religious mission had yet to fully establish its influence over the tribe. Nonetheless, both he and Oacpicagigua, though without tribal authorized decision-making power, were provoked by similar circumstances to plot against the Spaniards. Their resort to rebellion provided positive action leading to a regaining of traditional respect and a return to the old ways.

Calling the northern revolts merely a reaction to economic changes as the northern frontier modernized ignores the fact that, at first, the question of colonial expansion concerned Indian leaders only slightly as they enjoyed attention from military men, missionaries, and vecinos vying for their services. Their accommodation to the outsiders lost value as they observed missionary efforts to organize their people under Indians not having authorized control in the traditional tribal sense. Such interference with the Indian socio-politico-religious structure antagonized several and spurred them to violent rebellion. Encouraged by the intertribal outlook of their lieutenants, a highly capable Indian leadership resolutely acted to remove the encroaching colonial influence. In that regard, Salvador Palma succeeded.

But, like Bernabé and Muni of the Yaqui people, Salvador Palma sought to serve as a buffer between his followers and the Spaniards. Apparently, all three leaders had developed a zone of autonomy within the evolving northern frontier. That they could, and did, directly bargain with the viceroy in Mexico City obviously gave them power to manage their personal freedoms. Yet they lost their encounter, or preservation of power, as the nature of Spanish bureaucracy responded to them. Thus, they took part in an age-old drama of community uprooting, transforming, and surviving.

CHAPTER VII

FOOTNOTES

¹A nephew of the Marqués de Croix, Teodoro de Croix troubleshot for the crown. Born near Lille, France in 1730, his long and distinguished career in the Spanish army began with his enlistment at seventeen. He served as an officer of the Grenadiers of the Royal guard, later transferring to the Walloon Guard. In 1756, he received his title of caballero when given the cross of the Teutonic Order for valorous service in Flanders. His career as a military administrator began in Mexico and Cuba; his appointment to the Provincias Internas was in recognition of his personal merit and probable ability to solve Spain's troublesome Indian problem and prevent foreign agression from the north. Alfred B. Thomas, Thoedoro de Croix and the Northern Frontier of New Spain, 1776-1783, 17-18.

²King Charles III to Croix, Real Instrucción, San Ildefonso, August 22, 1776, AGN, PI 77, expedient 4. For a published copy of this important document, see Velasco Ceballos, La administracion de D. Frey Antonio María de Bucareli, 1: 332-42.

³Thomas, Teodoro de Croix, 20-21, 28-29; Bobb, The Viceregency of Antonio María Bucareli, 146-47.

⁴Anza to Croix, Horcasitas, May 23, 1777, AGI, Guadalajara 516; Díaz, Diario de operaciones, Río Florido, May 28 and 31, 1777, AGI, Guadalajara 515; Barri to Croix, Durango, June 28 and July 5, 1777, AGI, Guadalajara 515.

⁵Croix to Gálvez, Nos. 90-93, Querétaro, August 23, 1777, AGI, Guadalajara 516; Croix to Gálvez, Nos. 95-97, Mexico, August 23, 1777, AGI, Guadalajara 515.

⁶This conflict climaxed in confrontation between Father Junípero Serra and Governor Felipe de Neve, due in part to the intransigent nature of both men. The issue was Franciscan autonomy in setting goals and conducting their affairs in the province without interference from a reformist administration. See for example, Bucareli to Felipe de Neve, Mexico, September 30, 1774, AGN, PI 166; Junípero Serra to Croix, Santa Bárbara, April 28, 1778, AGN, California 1, 2; Neve to Croix, Monterey, March 26, 1781, AGN, California 2, 1; Neve, Instrucción, Saucillo, September 7, 1782, paragraphs 1-5, AGI, Guadalajara 283.

⁷Moorhead, The Apache Frontier, 49-51; John, Storms Brewed in Other Men's Worlds, 488-89.

⁸A certified copy of the proceedings appears as enclosure No. 1 in Croix to Gálvez, No. 217 and Croix to Gálvez, Nos. 236-39, Chihuahua, July 27, 1779, AGI, Guadalajara 276. See also Thomas, Teodoro de Croix, 36-44. Detailed examination of the earlier councils is in Herbert E. Bolton, ed., Athanase de Mézieres and the Louisiana-Texas Frontier, 1768-1780, 2: 152-70.

⁹Gálvez to Croix, El Pardo, February 20, 1779 (certified copy enclosed with Royal Order of 1779), AGN, PI 170, expediente 5; Croix to Gálvez, No. 458, Informe General, Arizpe, January 23, 1780, paragraph I, AGI, Guadalajara 278.

¹⁰Charles E. Chapman, A History of California: The Spanish Period, 294-301.

¹¹Bucareli to Arriaga, No. 1421, Mexico, June 26, 1774, in Herbert E. Bolton, ed., Anza's California Expeditions, 5: 175-82.

¹²For a description of the Yuma nation and the most definitive study of the Yuma Revolt, see Jack D. Forbes, Warriors of the Colorado: The Yumas of the Quechan Nation and Their Neighbors.

¹³The San Diego revolt involved a large number of Indian bands who even asked the participation of their distant relatives, the Yumas. During the revolt, they killed three people, wounded eight, and burned the mission to the ground. Bucareli to Arriaga No. 2186, Mexico, March 27, 1776, in Bolton, Anza's California Expeditions, 5: 336-42.

¹⁴Anza to Bucareli, Mexico, November 20, 1779, in Bolton, Anza's California Expeditions, 5: 383-94. For Francisco Garcés's plan for the Yumas, see Scott Jarvis Maughan, "Francisco Garcés and New Spain's Northwestern Frontier, 1768-1781," unpublished Ph.D. dissertation, University of Utah, 1968, 199-257. For a biographical sketch of Garcés, see John L. Kessell, "The Making of a Martyr: The young Francisco Garcés," NMHR 45 (July 1970): 181-96. See also Juan Domingo Arricivita, Crónica Seráfica y Apostólica del Colegio de Propaganda fide de la Santa Cruz de Querétaro de la Nueva España (Mexico,1792), 489-514.

¹⁵Anza to Burareli, Mexico, November 20, 1776, in Bolton, Anza's California Expeditions, 5: 385-86.

¹⁶Ibid.

¹⁷Croix to Gálvez, No. 8 (reservado), Informe General, Arizpe, October 30, 1781, paragraphs 517-52, AGI, Guadalajara 253. For an English translation of this report, see Thomas, Teodoro de Croix, 71-243. Bucareli to Gálvez, No. 2793, Mexico, February 24, 1777, AGI, Guadalajara 516.

¹⁸Palma to Bucareli, Mexico, November 11, 1776, in Bolton, Anza's California Expeditions, 5: 365-77.

¹⁹Ibid., 373.

²⁰Royal title of appointment, Aranjuez, May 19, 1777, in Thomas, Forgotten Frontiers, 115-19.

²¹Bucareli to Gálvez, No. 2592, Mexico, November 26, 1776, in Bolton, Anza's California Expeditions, 5: 395-97; Forbes, Warriors of the Colorado, 181.

22Kessell, Friars, Soldiers, and Reformers, 138.

23Forbes, Warriors of the Colorado, 182-83.

24Arricivita, Cronica Seráfica y Apostólica, 502. Born in Italy in 1745, Santiago de Islas arrived in New Spain in the 1760s and worked up through the ranks of the Dragoon Regiment of Mexico. He campaigned against the Apaches in Sonora but fought in no encounters. Though a novice, Islas had a clean military record, and Commandant General Croix placed confidence in his ability. Islas, Hoja de servicios, December 31, 1780, AGI, Guadalajara 281.

25Croix, Extracto de Novedades, Arizpe, February 28, 1782 (enclosed with Croix to Gálvez, same place and date), AGI, Guadalajara 517; Arricivita, Crónica Seráfica y Apostólica, 496-502.

26Croix to Gálvez, No. 8 (reservado) Informe General, Arizpe, October 30, 1781, paragraphs 526-52, AGI, Guadalajara 253.

27Ibid.

28Croix, Extracto de Novedades, Arizpe, February 28, 1782 (enclosed with Croix to Gálvez, same place and date), AGI Guadalajara 517.

29Juan Domingo Arricivita, a Franciscan chronicler with access to Garcés's papers, wrote that civilian settlers arriving on the Colorado sought out prime land for themselves, usurping Indian fields, and grazed their horses, cattle, and sheep on the best lands, destroying Indian crops. Yumas resisted, but any sedition was quelled by the soldiers. Arricivita, Cronica Seráfica y Apostólica, 503-504; Santiago Islas to Croix, Diario de operaciones, Concepción, January 1, 1781, AGI, Guadalajara 517.

30Islas to Croix, Concepción, January 17, 1781, AGI, Guadalajara 517.

31Islas to Croix, Concepción, June 6, 1781, AGI, Guadalajara 517.

32Forbes, Warriors of the Colorado, 195-204.

33Ibid., 203-204.

34Jacobo Ugarte y Loyola, born in Spain around 1717, enrolled as a cadet in the Spanish army in 1732; he later served in the Italian and Portuguese campaigns. Promoted to colonel in 1767, Ugarte was sent to New Spain as governor of Coahuila. He also governed Sonora (1779-1782) and Puebla (1782-1786). In 1786, now Brigadier General Ugarte was appointed commandant general of the Provincias Internas, a post he held until 1790 when he became field marshal and governor-intendant of Guadalajara. He died there on August 20, 1798. Moorhead, The Apache Frontier, 19-63; Francisco R. Almada, Diccionario de historia, geografia y biografia sonorenses, 801-802, says Ugarte was born in the province of Guipuzcoa in 1728 and began his military career on April 15, 1742 in the Royal Infantry, having obtained an age waiver.

[35]Croix to Jacobo Ugarte, Arizpe, September 16, 1781, AGN, Historia 24.

[36]Croix to Gálvez, Nos. 718-20, Arizpe, February 28, 1782, AGI, Guadalajara 517.

[37]Croix to Gálvez, Arizpe, January 23, 1783, AGI, Guadalajara 518; Moorhead, The Apache Frontier, 59; Forbes, Warriors of the Colorado, 207-220.

[38]Croix to Gálvez, Arizpe, February 28, 1782, AGI Guadalajara 517.

[39]Ugarte to the Marqués de Sonora (José de Gálvez), Chihuahua, December 21, 1786, in Thomas, Forgotten Frontiers, 364-65; Petition of Anza to the King, Santa Fe, November 18, 1786, in Thomas, Forgotten Frontiers, 366-68.

[40]Croix to Gálvez, Arizpe, February 28, 1782, AGI, Guadalajara 517; Croix to Gálvez, Nos. 844-45, Arizpe, November 4, 1782, AGI, Guadalajara 517.

[41]Kessell, Friars, Soldiers, and Reformers, 146.

CHAPTER VIII

SERI, TARAHUMARA, AND GILENO RESISTANCE

In 1783, the former governor of California, Felipe de Neve, replaced Teodoro de Croix as commandant general. Neve's previous frontier experience, most notably against the Yumas in 1782, and his confidence in Croix's policies continued the Bourbon continuity during the year before his untimely death on August 21, 1784.[1] During his administration, Mescalero and Lipán Apaches continued their hit-and-run raiding in Coahuila, Gileños increased raids into Sonora, and Tarahumara renegades struck from out of the rugged recesses of the Sierra Madre, but the Seris of Sonora required Neve's immediate attention. After inspecting frontier defenses, Neve measured his adversary and concluded that the Seris and their Tiburón and Tepoca kinsmen needed to be soundly defeated for lasting example to be set in Sonora. But the Seris and their allies proved more elusive than the Tarahumaras, Mescaleros, and Lipánes. They only infrequently gathered in large numbers or stood and fought, and they carefully kept their rancherías from discovery, thus avoidinq surprise attacks by presidials or militia units. Even more so than their Nueva Vizcaya and Coahuila kinsmen, they possessed skills and instincts that made them extremely difficult to take at a disadvantage. Nevertheless, Neve marshalled his military resources to subjugate or exterminate Seri criminals.[2]

Royal orders of May 23. 1780, and March 2 and 6 of 1782 also called for vigorous persecution of the Seri, Tiburón, and Tepoca rebels, and after a war council of December 2. 1783, Neve resolved to congregate them at the Villa de Seris, across the river from Pitic. He intended to support them with weekly rations of food and other welfare necessities and, if necessary, deport any recalcitrants to Mexico City. Once there, their fate could be decided by the viceroy, provided it did not allow their return home. This policy of extermination of Seris averse to military pacification, weeding out of Indian leaders protesting internment of their people, and government subsidies for those submitting to reservation life, succeeded. By the spring of 1784, several Seri bands sued for peace and settled in the reservation-like communities near Pitic. Though some rebel bands still roamed freely, about seventy Seri families momentarily submitted peacefully.[3]

But Villa de Seris festered with factional intrigue, both within and between Spanish, mestizo, and Indian communities, the currents of discord overlapping, merging, and intermingling in confused ebb and flow. Abominable food rations and equally disgusting living conditions angered the Seris as the prospect of death or disability from disease increased at the camp. In addition, boredom mixed with the influence from rebel Seris further portended trouble. Growing numbers of vecinos surrounding the internment camp, contributed to the discontent by intruding on Seri lands and diverting water from the Río Sonora on which the precious Seri crops depended. On March 19, 1784, the frustrated Seris abandoned Villa de Seris and fled to the mountains, and the stage was set for another military struggle against loss of land and autonomy.[4]

The revolt's origins involved misunderstanding, land disputes, and strained relations between Indian and suspicious vecinos, but the truth is that despite the professions of peace, most Seris refused to abide by temporal or missionary rules. Though not averse to receiving annuity issues on the reserve or living there during the hard winter months, few wanted to settle permanently within the regulated lines marked out by the king's representatives. Their innate wanderlust had yet to be checked either by presidials or their own leaders.[5]

Unfortunately, Boquinete, their most powerful chieftain and a battlewise leader with a penetrating ability to expose frontier pretenses, died in 1779, during a presidial attack on the Cerro Prieto. Two leaders rose to fill his place, and they exerted strong regional influence in coordinating hit-and-run resistance.[6] Commandant General Neve proved unsuccessful at bringing Indian warriors to battle. From March through May, the army recorded 10 unit actions with Sonoran Indians and claimed a kill of 26 at a cost of 12 Spanish deaths and recovery of 36 head of Spanish livestock. At the same time, Indian raiders stole 1,116 head of livestock, destroyed many cattle ranches and farms, took a copious amount of war booty, kept the Bolaños de Plata mine of northern Sonora from full operation, causing severe economic hardship to the province. As hostilities continued, Seri bands joined forces with Gileños of Pimería Alta, fled to Tiburón Island, or drifted back to the religious missions. Still others persisted in menacing agrarian/livestock centers and making road travel in northwestern Sonora a risky venture.[7]

In March of 1784. Neve returned to his long-awaited counter-offensive against Gileño Apache rebels, determined against any temporizing with the enemy. Drawing from the garrisons of Nueva Vizcaya, Sinaloa, and Sonora, he built a five division force of about eight hundred veteran troops. Neve saw success dependent on striking at the heart of their sierra strongholds. He assured Gálvez that he would not only continue the war against the enemy as specified in the royal ordinances, "but will mount a continuous offensive . . . . not allowing them the time to regroup in distant hideaways."[8] But aside from the victories of the Opata Indian companies of Bavispe and Bacoachi, the spring offensive only moderately succeeded. Arriving in Fronteras in early June, Neve totaled the results: 68 Indians killed, 17 captured, 168 horses and mules recovered, and a large quantity of buffalo and deer skins confiscated.[9]

Neve believed this kind of campaign would bring the rebels to terms, but no other detachment enjoyed the same measure of success. The Gileños, division of the Chiricahuas loosely embracing the Mimbreño, Salinero, and Mogollón groups, continued their devastating raids in Sonora. The commandant general received reports from Nueva Vizcaya that a Tarahumara, Antonio Hernández (alias el Mordullo), assembling a large force of Indians in the Sierra Mojada, was exhorting them to step up hit-and-run raiding in that province. The most heavily attacked jurisdictions included Cuencamé, San Juan del Río. Santa Bárbara, San José del Parral , and Real de Oro. Equally if not more important news came that Mescalero and Lipán bands in Coahuila had also been aroused. These hostilities forced Neve to terminate the Gila campaign and focus his efforts on Nueva Vizcaya and Coahuila.[10]

Neve turned his attention in Nueva Vizcaya to the deteriorating situation among the Tarahumaras. They had not staged an uprising since 1690, but Tarahumara loyalty had long been suspect, and Neve believed that immediate trial and execution of those rebels already imprisoned at Chihuahua would serve as an example to other Indian renegades. The commandant general fully opposed any gentle treatment of Tarahumara war-criminals. In March of 1784, he sentenced Juan Felipe de Jesús from Encino de la Paz and Antonio Moreno, a casta from the agrarian center of Naicha, to death by hanging for collaborating with Apaches. Soon after, other rebels, Ignacio de Díos and José Armendariz (father and son) from the pueblo of Nonvada, Andrés de la Cruz from Crichic, Jaime el Cojo from Norogachic, Juan Marcial from San José de Bacuiachiz, and Manta Prieta from Cueva all received the same sentence. After the execution, the quartered bodies were placed on the highway through Chihuahua, and the heads went on display at the center of the victims' village birthplaces.[11]

To be caught and killed while committing highway robbery or plundering a hacienda or mine was one thing, but to stand trial for war crimes against the crown was quite another. Tarahumara renegades understood nothing about such alien concepts as summary justice or capital punishment. Further, though the frontier military blundered through one protracted campaign after another, able to penetrate Tarahumara hideaways only with the help of Indian auxiliaries, they had yet to win any decisive victory over the renegades. To the Tarahumaras, the Neve trials and executions only appeared illogical. The special fate of the Indian war criminals, unthinkable in its savagery, shocked them and resulted in stepped-up harassment of frontier settlements. Neve later exercised greater caution when sentencing twenty-one other prisoners of war, ordering execution of only two--Santiago Felipe, a Tarahumara, and the mestizo Matías Gomez. The commandant general deemed this an opportune time to end the deteriorating situation causing Nueva Vizcaya's ruin. He reported that the prisons were full of criminals, "and there are still many cimarrón bands, especially around the jurisdictions of Cienega de los Olivos and Cusihuiriachic, that are still at liberty to aid the enemy."[12] Neve commissioned Lieutenant Colonel Manuel Múñoz to find and gather the dispersed Tarahumara bands and persuade them to surrender as temporary hostages until arrangement of a meaningful treaty. Múñoz and four detachments of troops, though never getting close enough for negotiation, skirmished with the rebels a few times, destroying a sizeable ranchería and capturing thirty-five prisoners, mostly women and children. The remaining rebels split into small parties and fled deeper into the mountains or drifted back to their mission villages.[13]

Seemingly pleased with the results of the campaign, Neve reported on May 31, 1784, that since initiation of the Tarahumara offensive, the Apaches had been stripped of their most trusted allies and their raiding had declined in the province. With the prison at Chihuahua overloaded, Neve no longer interned Tarahumara criminals there, resolving instead to overlook their misdeeds and place them on a reservation on the outskirts of the villa. Preventing their leaving the confines of the internment camp, Neve would offer them the same arrangement as mission Indians and, if they agreed to stop their highway banditry, he would allow missionaries among them.[14]

Nothing guaranteed a binding agreement with the Tarahumaras for their war spirit still persisted, and Nueva Vizcaya remained threatened. Indian rebels continued attacking isolated ranches, agrarian centers, and mining camps. But on Neve's initiative, Lieutenant Colonel Múñoz at least isolated some troublemakers at internment camps near Chihuahua. Neve never witnessed the outcome of his efforts since after six months of suffering the ravages of dysentery, he died at the hacienda de Nuestra Señora de Carmen while enroute from Arizpe to Chihuahua.15

Neve's temporary successor, Colonel José Antonio Rengel continued the policy of pursuing Tarahumara renegades and in November of 1784, reported approximately 900 prisoners of war interned at Chihuahua and Durango. But Colonel Rengel stayed all orders of execution, giving himself time to examine more humane means of pacifying the frontier area. Rengel saw no further necessity to continue the hangings, believing the reason for the problems in Nueva Vizcaya to be Tarahumara abandonment of their rancherías to work on landed estates. "They then become uprooted and are susceptible to collaboration with the enemy and highway robbery in order to survive."16   Lacking other orders, Rengel granted amnesty to Tarahumaras voluntarily seeking it, dependent on their promise to live under military protection on assigned reservations near Chihuahua where they would receive weekly rations until they became self-sufficient.

A year later, Rengel dispatched Captain Juan Bautista Elguezábal with 120 troops to inspect the Tarahumara country and round up any remaining criminals and other renegades hiding in their rancherías. In a four-month campaign, Captain Elguezábal visited 79 missions and villages, and 16 haciendas, apprehending 71 war criminals and 41 mission renegades. After another unauthorized campaign that netted 49 mission fugitives, the remaining rebels sued for peace. Rengel demanded that the Indians allow missionaries in their villages or accept the authority of a principal chief, cease wandering and surrender all mixed-blood allies, and permit royal commissioners in their villages at least twice a year. Such peace requirements ended Rengel's efforts to stop Tarahumara banditry in Nueva Vizcaya. Whether Rengel's moves helped or hindered the war effort is unclear for his successor received more specific instructions on dealing with the Tarahumara renegades. Incoming Commandant General Pedro de Nava would be one of several military officials to conclude a Tarahumara peace.17

In August of 1784, over three hundred Gileño, Pima, and Pápago rebels attacked presidio San Agustín de Tucson in Sonora; at Bacoachi, two hundred Apaches killed eight frontiersmen, among them Francisco Tomohua, captain of the Opata company from that village; and the horse herd of Fronteras suffered two hit-and-run raids. The tide of war turned against Rengel, and in the fall of 1784, he dispatched under Captain Manuel de Echegaray a force of two hundred and ten presidials, plus the Indian companies of Bavispe and San Ignacio, to do battle in the sierras of Las Rastras and Peñascosa. The campaign, save the successes of the Pima and Opata companies, failed.18

Like Neve, Rengel believed that dealing effectively with Indian rebels in Sonora meant rooting out the hostiles from their ranchería hideaways, despite possible violations of friendly tribes' territories. After a particularly bloody raid in fall of 1784, Rengel instructed Captain Manuel Azuela to rout the offenders from their sierra strongholds. In early March of 1785, Azuela returned from the unsuccessful two-month campaign in the Sierra de Chiricahui. In the same month, a detachment of troops--Ensign Domingo de Vergara with eighty soldiers from Bavispe, Bacoachi, and Fronteras--smashed a renegade ranchería of about a hundred Apache and mixed-bloods near the presidio of Fronteras. Rengel continued using small unit offensives in enemy territory but launched only one effective major offensive. In extended winter campaigning, his forces killed only fourteen Indians, recovered twenty-seven head of stock, and lost one soldier and over fifty of their own animals.[19]

The 1785 offensive achieved little because many presidio commanders, especially Captain Pedro de Allande y Saavedra of San Agustín del Tucson, refused to operate in general campaigns that left their presidios undefended.[20] And Comandant General Rengel, gravely ill with diarrhea, could not personally direct military operations. Viceroy Matías de Gálvez died on November 3, 1784, and no immediate orders emanated from Mexico City, leaving the temporary Rengel administration at an impasse.[21]

Bernardo de Gálvez assumed the viceroyalty of New Spain in June of 1785, approaching the Indian problem with a practicality that reconciled the reorganization aims of the past. Deeply frustrated by the previous futile attempts to secure the frontier against a shadow enemy,Viceroy Gálvez took a harder view of his opponent. His Instrucción de 1786 stated that if a tribe or band failed to restrain raids on frontier settlements, the whole group became public enemies to be hunted and punished accordingly. Ignoring Indian social and political organization, Gálvez followed the erroneously established principle that tribal leaders possessed full authority to negotiate treaties.[22] Such theory held definite advantages for presidio captains since it enabled them to define and recognize an enemy, wage quasi-war against him; more importantly, it potentially offered them conqueror status. Severe enough punishment of the group, innocent suffering along with guilty, might indeed produce true group responsibility and bring peace to the frontier and power to the presidio commander. Neither the Reglamento of 1772 nor conditions of frontier service ever changed fundamentally, and the monotony of garrison life relieved occasionally by profitless patrols and pursuits still characterized duty at the presidios.[23]

Still, confusion and uncertainty characterized Spain's Indian policy, and particularly the roles played by the viceroy and commandant general. But after 1786, the autonomy of the commandancy suffered from a reorganization that blurred lines of authority and made firm central direction difficult. Despite the effectiveness of Viceroy Gálvez's Indian policy, his instructions to Commandant General Ugarte as well as Indian relations suffered from the breakdown in coordination that accompanied administrative reorganization following his death.[24]

The presidials' record during this period of uncertainty is found in the resúmenes de las muertos y robos (monthly battle reports), compiled from the reports of front line officers and submitted by the commandant generals to their superiors. Gaps exist in these reports, tallies being only educated guesses accompanied by the usual war time exaggeration of body counts. But lacking similar Indian documents, the estimates do give some indication of wins and losses.

From February 1778 to June 1796, the resúmenes show casualties inflicted by both sides about equal. Enemy warriors killed 2,069 frontier people, mostly vecinos, while Spain's frontier forces killed 2,004 Indians, mostly warriors. Indians took 279 captives (mostly mestizos and castas) while the troops captured 1,808 Indians (mostly women and children). Indians, especially the Apaches, made significant gains in the theft of Spanish livestock. They reportedly stole 41,519 head (mostly horses and mules), but the troops recovered only 18,550--considerably less than half their losses.[25] During the years mentioned, figures vary little, either in trend or in combined casualties. No advantages gained by either side are indicated which shows a remarkable record of sustained and continuous rebellion. Had they capitulated, Indians of New Spain's northern frontier would have gone the way of many of Mexico's Indian peoples, preserved in the history books.

CHAPTER VIII

FOOTNOTES

1Edwin A. Beilharz, Felipe de Neve, First Governor of California, 8-19, 140-41.

2Neve to Gálvez, No. 27, Arizpe, September 22, 1783, AGI, Guadalajara 267; Neve to Gálvez, No. 33, Arizpe, October 20, 1783, AGI, Guadalajara 518.

3Neve to Gálvez, No. 4, Arizpe, March 8, 1784, AGI, Guadalajara 519.

5Ibid.

6Croix, Extracto de Novedades, Arizpe, January 23, March 26, April 23, May 23, 1780 (enclosed with Croix to Gálvez, Nos. 461, 508, 528, same place and dates), AGI, Guadalajara 271.

7Neve, Extracto y resumen de hostilidades, Arizpe, March 8, April 5, 1784 (enclosed with Neve to Gálvez, Nos. 90, 98, same place and dates), AGI, Guadalajara 519; Neve, Extracto y resumen de hostilidades, Arizpe, May 31, 1784 (enclosed with Neve to Gálvez, No. 117, same place and date), AGI, Guadalajara 520.

8Neve to Gálvez, No. 91, Arizpe, March 8, 1784, AGI, Guadalajara 519.

9Neve, Extracto y resumen de hostilidades, Arizpe, July 6, 1784 (enclosed with Neve to Gálvez, No. 122, same place and date), AGI, Guadalajara 520.

10Ibid.

11Neve, Ocho reos de trato y coligación con los enemigos y otros excesos, Arizpe, March 8, 1784 (enclosed with Neve to Gálvez, No. 93, same place and date), AGI, Guadalajara 285.

12Neve, Noticias de la persecución de malhechores y de la pena capital que ha impuesto a varios de ellos, Arizpe, May 3, 1784 (enclosed with Neve to Gálvez, No. 112, same place and date), AGI, Guadalajara 285.

13Neve to Gálvez, No. 116, Arizpe, May 31, 1784, AGI, Guadalajara 285.

14Ibid.

15Navarro García, Don José de Gálvez, 443.

16Colonel José Antonio Rengel to Gálvez, No. 5, Chihuahua, November 27, 1784, AGI, Guadalajara 285; Rengel to the Marqués de Sonora (José de Gálvez), Nos. 138-39, Chihuahua, March 2, 1786, AGI, Guadalajara 286; Christon I. Archer, The Army in Bourbon Mexico, 1760-1810, 208.

[17]Navarro García, Don José de Gálvez, 449; Gálvez, Instrucción de 1786, Articles 125-35; Commandant General Pedro de Nava, Informe general de las Provincias Internas, Chihuahua, January 5, 1796, AGI, Guadalajara 586.

[18]Rengel, Extracto y resumen de hostilidades, Chihuahua, November 1, December 25, 1784 (enclosed with Rengel to Gálvez, Nos. 3, 12, same place and dates), AGI, Guadalajara 520.

[19]Rengel, Exracto y resumen de hostilidades, Chihuahua, February 26, March 26, April 30, 1785 (enclosed with Rengel to Gálvez, Nos. 28, 55, 68, same place and dates), AGI, Guadalajara 520; Rengel to the Marqués de Sonora, No. 141, Chihuahua, March 2, 1786, AGI, Guadalajara 286.

[20]Henry F. Dobyns, Spanish Colonial Tucson, 63, 89-91, 113-14.

[21]Rengel to Gálvez, No. 22, February 26, 1785, AGI, Guadalajara 268; Moorhead, The Presidio, 99.

[22]Gálvez, Instrucción de 1786, Articles 18-79.

[23]Bernardo de Gálvez's much publicized Instrucción synthesized past policies, mainly the recommendations of the Marqués de Rubí, the Reglamento of 1772, recommendations of various war councils, and the Royal Order of 1779. Viceroy Gálvez encouraged Commandant General Jacobo Ugarte to carry out a uniform policy of government welfare for tribes accepting peace and total war against recalcitrants. This approach, used repeatedly, now came close to bringing peace, but with the outbreak of the war for independence in 1810 and its diversion of troops and money, hostility flared. See John F. Park, "Spanish Indian Policy in Northern Mexico, 1765-1818," Arizona and the West 4 (Winter 1962): 340-44.

[24]Moorhead, The Presidio, 111-14.

[25]Moorhead, "The Soldado de Cuera," Journal of the West 8 (January 1969): 52.

CHAPTER IX

MILITARY DEFENSE
ON THE NORTHERN FRONTIER

Vast distance, climatic extremes, and scarce water, food, and fuel characterized New Spain's northern frontier and severely limited military policy. War with the hostile environment consumed as much of the total Bourbon effort as war with crime-committing Indians. Aggravating the situation was the Indians' near perfect accord with their environment which allowed them to turn the plains, mountains, and deserts of the north to their military advantage. Unlike their southern brethren, many northern Indians mounted wiry ponies as finely attuned with the environment as their riders. Also in contrast to the southern tribes, these semi- or wholly nomadic northern groups practiced only a ranchería lifeway that did not fix them for extended periods at predictable locations.

Commandant General Croix considered the horse warriors of the north a finer cavalry than his celebrated compañía volantes (light troops). "The first conquerors fought a people who had never seen a horse or gun," declared Croix, "but now the powerful Apaches, Comanches. and Nations of the North excel in horsemanship."[1] The individual warrior deserved the praise. He first used the horse for food but before long effectively put it to work in hunts and combat. Almost from infancy, the warrior devoted himself wholeheartedly to revolutionizing his way of life. Mounted or on foot, skilled with bow and arrows, lance, war club, and knife, he developed in himself qualities the commandant general hoped to inculcate in his light troops--an aggressive, warlike spirit, courage, physical strength and endurance, mental alertness, cunning, and thorough knowledge of the land and how to make full military use of it. Beyond this, the Indian warrior's highest values centered on success in war and the rewards--material, social, political, religious--it garnered. In training and in combat, he rarely lacked motivation.[2]

Croix's assessment cannot be extended, however. The northern Indian, though a first-rate light cavalryman, did not often function as a member of a first-rate combat unit of light cavalry. If individual ability attained high expression, group ability suffered severe limitations. According to Croix, the Indians' loose social and political organization exalted the individual at the expense of the group. "Each Indian," wrote Croix, "is a free republic who lives by hunting and thievery. Not one of them has a feel for the concept of nation."[3] Never was a tribe or band a monolithic entity with a leadership hierarchy controlling the actions of people. Indians, especially the Apache, practiced a democracy so extreme as to be incomprehensible to intruders. This led to endless friction with frontier commanders who wrongly assumed that since a chief commanded in battle, he could also force his followers to settle near a presidio and profess a peace binding on his people. Such constant misunderstanding underlay more than one rebellion, and many an innocent Indian leader suffered charges of bad faith from military officials who viewed Indian institutions from their own frame of reference.[4]

Croix's emphasis of the Indian warrior as a free republic expressed itself both in the objectives and methods of war. Instead of smashing the enemy and compelling his submission as in conventional warfare, the Indian fighter sought individual enrichment through booty accumulation and war honors earned by correct performance of culturally ordained feats. This held true whether the immediate cause of warfare was defense against invasion or raiding, revenge for casualties sustained in previous encounters, retaliation for real or imagined injuries, simple hit-and-run raids aimed at harassing frontier people, or even, as it became with the passage of time, tribal preservation.

A war party customarily numbered five to twenty men, sometimes more, and only rarely included the entire tribe or band. It set forth under the loose leadership of any warrior prestigious enough to enlist and organize one, and in the field, he commanded only to the extent that his followers chose to obey. Throughout the expedition, the group as well as each individual conscientiously performed required religious rituals and respected taboos to assure success of the mission. Unless the odds overwhelmingly favored success, warriors avoided close combat for casualties, regardless of the expedition's outcome, irreplaceably lessened their strength.[5]

The presidio soldier's field service, disadvantaged by the Indian's reluctance to stand and fight, unless his family was endangered, plus his mastery of guerrilla warfare, yielded one fruitless, disheartening pursuit after another. Skirmishes lasted no longer than it took the Indians to hit and run, and the rare large battles in the Provincias Internas usually resulted from a series of accidents or grave miscalculations by both Indians and soldier-settlers. Far more common was the experience lamented by Colonel Domingo Elizondo:

> Until the third battle of Cerro Prieto, we have ignored the worth of campaigning in such inaccessible mountains, but the other two offensives only penetrated Palma and Cara Pintada canyons . . . this time we have advanced to the heart of Cerro Prieto and managed to capture eleven Seris, kill eight, and take several prisoners, primarily women.[6]

Presidial companies provided Spanish frontier life some advantage. Distinct from Spain's regular soldiers, colonial militia, or special frontier units organized occasionally, the presidio troops usually incorporated settler-stockmen types (mestizos, mulatos, moriscos, coyotes, lobos, and castas) native to the frontier provinces. Mediocre as soldiers but accustomed to the unconventional tactics of Indian warfare, they had a natural capability born of a rugged existence, and when fighting as disciplined combat units instead of fragmenting for the Indian method of personal encounter, they won several striking victories. Many potential successes suffered logistical problems. Fighting against Apaches, Commandant Inspector O'Conor attempted to defeat them in an all-out campaign. The Apaches divided, each band battling separately and directing their efforts at eluding his troops rather than resisting them. As a result, O'Conor overextended his line of supplies and in fifteen encounters, beginning in late 1775, he killed 130 Apaches, captured 104 others, and recovered approximately two thousand horses and mules. In contrast, between 1771 and 1776, Apache raiders in Nueva Vizcaya alone killed 1,936 persons, captured 155 others, and stole 678,873 head of cattle, sheep, and goats.[7]

The inability of a tribe or group of tribes to unite for vigorous, sustained offense or defense gave Spanish frontiersmen another advantage. Their very existence as a people endangered by repeated military persecution, the northern tribes neither collectively nor individually presented a solid front of opposition for very long, nor did they respond with anything more original than the revolts of resistance in the traditional pattern. What does distinguish their resistance, however, is their remarkable endurance and persistence against the Spanish conquerors.

The nature of the terrain as well as that of the enemy dictated military requirements in the Provincias Internas. Vast, inhospitable land demanded either troops able to live off the country in the Indian manner or a supremely developed logistical system permitting operations independent of natural resources. Warring against a highly mobile enemy skilled in guerrilla tactics required either an equally mobile counterguerrilla force or a heavy defensive armed force large enough to erect an impenetrable shield of presidios around every settlement and travel route in the north. For reasons not wholly or even largely understood, presidials and citizen militia met these requirements. The performance of mobile companies in pursuit missions led to extended debate over the comparative efficiency of mixed-blood soldiery and infantry in punitive campaigns, but ultimately, front-line officers and men learned how to conduct operations against their Indian foe.[8]

Three tragedies dramatized the taxing requirements placed on presidial forces by both land and enemy. On September 26, 1774, Captain Manuel Alegre y Bohórquez with the 100-man Third Compañía Volante, 25 indios amigos, and a volunteer militia unit, pursued two bands of Indian raiders from the Valle de San Buenaventura. Alegre's command surprised them the following morning in the Sierra Escondida and after nine hours of pursuit killed two Indians and lost one soldier and ten horses. The warrior bands then split and fled. On September 29, Alegre overtook one of them in the San Joaquín Valley where he and his men were outfoxed. The enemy took the cover of a steep ridge, forcing the cavalry to dismount and attack on foot. Ensign Domingo Marañón with ten men and fifteen Suma infantrymen quickly followed Captain Alegre up the ridge; at the top, they discovered over one hundred Indian warriors in wait. They killed Alegre and three of his men outright and critically wounded Ensign Marañón and the others. The Suma captain was also critically hurt. Military command fell to Antonio Casimiro de Esparza, former Lieutenant governor of Sonora, who quickly directed a retreat.[9]

On October 2, Captain Nicolás Gil from the Real Presidio de San Buenaventura dispatched Ensign Manuel Villa with fifty troops to recover the bodies. But "his soldiers were so frightened that they did not want to dismount and investigate the scene of the battle."[10] The commandant inspector conducted a thorough investigation of the incident, and because of the actions at San Joaquín, Ensign Villa lost his commission, and Casimiro became captain of the Third Compañía Volante. A year later, Indian warriors used a similar tactic once again.

On a routine search and destroy patrol from Janos to San Buenaventura, Casimiro and 14 troops met their death at the hands of 300 Apache warriors.[11]

Furious, the officers and men of the Third Compañía Volante sought to avenge the death of their two commanders. On April 26, 1776, near the ranch of Becerras, while on a routine patrol over the same fatal terrain, Ensign Narciso Tapia with 42 troops maneuvered a force of 300 Apaches into five hours of a running battle, killing 40 at a loss of 6 killed and 29 wounded. Even more costly than the Becerras victory came a shocking defeat suffered on July 7 by the garrison of Santa Cruz de Terrenate in which Captain Francisco Tovar and 25 presidial died in pursuit of a band of Gileño rebels. Later investigation placed responsibility for the disaster on the negligence of Captain Tovar.[12] Still, these episodes reinforced the presidial companies' reputation for lethargy and ineffectiveness; but year after year, as frontier clashes continued without letup, a civilian populace tormented by murder, property loss, and constant insecurity was somehow protected by frontier forces that beat back Indian hostilities.

The presidio--this essential element of military organization in northern New Spain--not only assured Spanish hegemony and protection of the vecinos but also participated in their development. Yet it had stature only in relation to the quality of its manpower. Since little variance existed, any frontier garrison could serve to typify them, but events at the Real Presidio de San Buenaventura in September of 1774 make it exemplary.

San Buenaventura was founded in 1765 to cope with the spreading hostility in Nueva Vizcaya and was situated in the Valle de San Buenaventura to bolster the sagging presidio defenses. Relocated northward to the Valle de Velarde in early 1774 as part of Hugo O'Conor's general reorganization of the frontier line, it was later removed by Teodoro de Croix thirty-two miles to a site known as Chavarría (present Galeana, Chihuahua) to better defend the settlements of Valle de San Buenaventura.[13]

The extent of San Buenaventura's manpower is found in the Revista de Inspección of Commandant Inspector O'Conor's dealing with inspection of that presidio on January 26, 1774. The report lists the garrison's supplies as well as records for each soldier noting edad (age), patria (place of birth), robustez (general health), calidad (social background), and circunstancias (state of affairs). This information, incorporated into statistical tables, went to the crown.[14]

San Buenaventura had a captain, lieutenant, sergeant, four corporals, and thirty-eight soldiers but lacked both ensign and chaplain. Its commander, a young frontier line officer, Captain Nicolás Gil, started his military career on July 29, 1762. Enlisting as a private in the garrison of El Norte, he served eight years, quickly worked up through the ranks, achieving captaincy on March 15, 1771, and appointment as military commandant for Nueva Vizcaya in 1778. While Adjutant Inspector Diego de Borica considered him an excellent Indian campaigner, he reported that Captain Gil had little zeal for the management of his company.[15] Representative of presidio commanders who could not be both administrator and field officer, Gil apparently chose the latter.

Typically, the enlisted force of San Buenaventura came from frontier settler-stockmen types native to the north. The neighboring community of San Buenaventura supplied most of the personnel for the garrison, while also maintaining a citizen militia of fifty volunteers. The garrison included eighteen native San Buenaventurans, six El Pasoans, and three New Mexicans. Except for the New Mexicans, all of the enlisted force were born relatively close to the presidio. Rarely did frontiersmen journey great distances to serve in frontier garrisons, so local vecinos comprised most presidial companies.[16]

Noncommissioned officers formed the backbone of the enlisted force. Sergeant Mariano Montaño, a tough but paternalistic veteran, Corporals Juan Ignacío Gonzalez, José Antonio Marrufo, Ignacío Garisuain, and Alberto Barela all had experience in Indian campaigns. They personified the esprit de corps of presidial service but also received severe criticism for their so-called neglect of duty. Yet they contributed certain strengths to San Buenaventura. Four of the five were literate, relieving Captain Gil and Lieutenant Francisco Trujillo of much tedious paper work, and they excelled in discipline, morale, and physical endurance. Above all , they performed well on campaign and in combat.[17]

The notations on age and social background revealingly display the character of the company. Classification at San Buenaventura included twenty-three españoles (offspring of casta and Spaniard), six indios (Indian and coyote), five mestizos (Spaniard and Indian), five mulatos (Spaniard and Black), one lobo (Black and Indian), and one New Mexican, Juan Lucero, labeled mediana ("middle"). The oldest soldier was forty-nine; the youngest, eighteen-year-old Juan Antonio Chacón, had less than a year of presidio service. Average age at San Buenventura was just under thirty.[18]

The company of San Buenaventura discouraged Indian raiding parties, but failed to discourage the restless push of settlers. The garrison implied security and markets for produce, hastening the advance of the settlements in the Valle de San Buenaventura. Two years after Commandant Inspector O'Conor relocated it, the recent arrivals left that presidio and demanded a new one. San Buenaventura's relocation resulted as much from scarcities of wood, pasture, and water as from unsanitary conditions at the garrison. Improper diet led to malnutrition and stomach disorders caused by the polluted water supply.[19]

Once resituated at Chavarría, San Buenaventura became both a chartered town and military garrison, and social life of the villa and presidio followed an unvarying military pattern. Until election of a cabildo, municipal administration fell to Captain Gil. Military rank ordered the official and social hierarchy of San Buenaventura, determining authority, privileges, and social standing of both military and civilian residents. The social ladder imposed rank on families of officers and common soldiers, whose existence the Reglamento of 1772 recognized, as well as the vecinos and Indian employees, also officially recognized. The common foot soldier occupied the bottom rung and Captain Gil the top, but the social mobility allowed among commissioned and noncommissioned officers often led to blood or marriage relationships between the two. These circumstances caused difficulty in adhering to the regulated routine of military life.[20]

Not surprisingly, Indian warriors quickly learned the military routine of San Buenaventura. Indian spies, day laborers for the garrison, readily sold information to any renegade band willing to purchase it. Officers and men of the presidio rarely altered their daily pattern; their offensive record against Indian hostiles was average. Thus, with only slight changes in mundane detail, San Buenaventura exemplifies the military enterprise against Indian rebels on the northern frontier.[21]

Though Bourbon officials sharply criticized O'Conor's administration, standard offensive methods remained unthreatened. Presidial companies, locked in the chain of forts and slow-moving lines of supply, crawled about the inhospitable northern vastness searching for an elusive enemy able to scatter and vanish instantly.[22] Such presidial operations tallied an impressive record of failure but succeeded often enough to discourage serious analysis of their validity. Most experienced officers knew their foe's mastery of guerrilla warfare, and many suggested using the same techniques against him. A few, specifically Croix and his immediate successor, Felipe de Neve, even elaborated an advantageous doctrine combining two kinds of warfare. Brigadier Neve suggested offsetting the enemy's advantages by using a campaign force with the quietest, most inconspicuous supply train possible to avoid alerting the enemy. He believed newly created companies of indios amigos ideal for the purpose since they marched and maneuvered on foot, required few pack animals for their meager provisions, and knew familiarly the habits, ideas, and languages of enemy tribes.[23]

Besides Commandant General Neve, military officials and northern governors regularly advocated recruitment of Indian volunteers for presidial service, and Croix himself created two new Sonora garrisons at San Ignacio with eighty-four Pimas and at Bavispe with eighty-four Opatas. Some military leaders opposed these efforts because Indian soldiers supposedly lacked discipline and enjoyed excessive violence and plundering. Croix's scheme and Neve's implementation involved lessening these disadvantages by incorporating the Indian garrisons directly under the command of veteran officers. A notable test of such a plan, the newly-formed Opata company of Bacoachi, yielded encouraging results. Led by Lieutenant José Varela, Ensign Eduardo Barri (son of the late governor of Nueva Vizcaya), and two veteran sergeants, they distinguished themselves in a major offensive against Gila Apaches in the spring of 1784. In the only moderately successful campaign, the Opata garrison of Bavispe managed to inflict most of the damage. "Being on foot," observed Neve, "they fought with extraordinary valor in a terrain which could not be reached by horseback or by other manner of troopers."[24]

Not an original idea, use of Indians against Indians finds precedent in Hernán Cortés's use of Indian allies against the armies of Montezuma as well as Viceroy Antonio de Mendoza's commissioning Aztec, Tlaxcalan, Tarascan, and other Indian allies during the Mixtón War of 1541-42. As noted earlier, Viceroy Luis de Velasco in the 1550s, employed Indian auxiliaries against the Chichimecas. The celebrated Reglamento of 1772 authorized squads of indios amigos for each presidio, and the use of Pueblo Indian auxiliaries in New Mexico points out emphatically to their worth. Neve valued indios amigos not only as effective scouts, interpreters, and presidial reinforcements but as daring soldiers as well. Organized in military units under veteran officers, they functioned as regular troops in vulnerable areas, fighting with cunning, stealth, and endurance equalling that of the foe. Even as the commandant general wrote, Opata soldiers of Bavispe and Bacoachi, and Pimas from the relocated company of San Ignacio validated his thesis, proving conclusively their effectiveness as organized presidial companies.[25]

Viceroy Bernardo de Gálvez also viewed Indian warfare with a rare insight.[26] Like Neve, he understood the advantages of smaller troop detachments for offensive campaigns. A force of only 150 to 200 soldiers reduced the required number of horses and mules, aroused less suspicion and still sufficed militarily for the campaign. Gálvez also suggested substitution of lower paid indios amigos for some of the presidios of Nueva Vizcaya, New Mexico, Sinaloa, and Sonora to reduce military expenses. He instructed his three major officers, Jacobo Ugarte, Juan de Ugalde, and José Antonio Rengel to form alliances with every band or tribe seeking peace and array them against those still at war. The officers had a difficult assignment since Indian auxiliaries generally fought under their own leaders, following their own inclinations as often as instructions from officers accompanying them.[27]

Commandant General Ugarte varied Galvez's orders. Rather than pitting one tribe against another, he sought allies from within the very tribe he fought. This efficacious strategy successfully matched the enemy's special skills and overwhelmed him psychologically as he saw some of his own arrayed against him. In the spring of 1787, the Comanche, Ute, Jicarilla and Navajo nations not only made peace but also enlisted as auxiliaries against warring Apache renegades. Ugarte secured peace with Chiricahua Apaches in Sonora and with Mescaleros and Lipánes in Nueva Vizcaya then began a total war against the Gileños of Pimería Alta. In all, some 4,200 Apaches and 3,000 of their Navajo kinsmen sued for peace while presidials and militia units systematically hunted down the remaining warring bands.[28]

Use of Indians as combat forces entailed grave risks. Kinship with the hunted people, racial if not tribal, tempered auxiliaries' reliability, but tried and tested principles often offset this danger. In 1787, using his kind of tactics, Ugarte convinced several Apaches to become scouts by sending seventeen recalcitrant warriors in chains to Guadalajara, retaining those more docile for military service. Both as scouts and auxiliaries, indios amigos compiled a uniform record, performing faithfully in small, poorly equipped, underpaid, badly coordinated units buffeted by the patronage politics that afflicted the military command in the late 1770s.[29]

The Reglamento of 1772 had fixed frontier man-strength at 910 officers and men, designating as well its composition, its military rules. Lack of numerical strength precluded reliance on static defense, and frontier commanders should have compensated for it with mobility. The agile enemy clearly demanded it. Croix pointed out in 1786:

> Unlike the presidio soldier, the Indian warriors are well mounted and most expert at horsemanship, and they appreciate horses more than they do their families. They save their best mounts for the war against us and do not use them until ready for battle. The horses

obey so well that they come only at the sound of their masters' voice.[30]

Croix attempted to work around royal requirements by reinforcing the garrisons with his new recruited tropa ligera (light troops), creating a second line of defense composed of militia-garrisoned towns, and employing the compañías volantes as mobile strike force to defend the interior should the enemy penetrate presidio defenses. The vast extent of the frontier and type of warfare presidios encountered mandated some sort of change. Croix contended that each soldier having to maintain four to eight horses restricted him in offensive warfare and reduced the mobility necessary for search and destroy missions. "To fight the enemy, one must be prudent, patient, and reflective, rather than tramping all about the countryside with a string of several horses. Soldiers must be freed from this burden."[31]

Even with Croix's changes, presidio service meant grinding monotony interrupted only infrequently. Presidials endured unrewarding field duty, long periods of hunger, thirst, and lack of sleep, plus the prospect of death or disability from disease, enemy action, or a constitution broken by exposure and improper diet. Frontier army service meant low pay, little chance of advancement or personal recognition, and for enlisted personnel, little or no military instruction and drill.[32] Though officers supposedly trained the troops, there never seemed time enough for either instruction or practice. Presidio service required performance of mundane duties that pulled soldiers away from the garrisons and persisting in a profession commonly held in contempt. Croix recalled:

> It is a sad burden the common soldier suffers. His low moral, ignorance, insubordination, and lack of military discipline, leave him prey to the common vices of this country, and force him into a servile position. He therefore lacks ambition and cares little for his weapons, or the care of them; nor does he care for his horse and saddle.[33]

Though unfair to the able officers and men whose love of military life outweighed other considerations, Croix's charge that presidios harbored the misfits of frontier society held some truth. He himself made little headway in enforcing the Reglamento of 1772 and of protecting economic sources of revenue for the Spanish crown.

The frustration of presidial service held for the soldier, boredom, impoverished living conditions, constant drudge labor, and deadening fatigue. But the prospects for meaningful combat or opportunity for distinction existed to make military life endurable. Fighting Indians at once everywhere and nowhere, recognizable as enemies only on rare occasions when actually caught plundering or acting aggressively, added to presidials' discouraging lives, but did not undermine their steadfastness. By contrast, the reality of the frontier and its Indian cultures necessarily postponed presidial success. Part of this reality was the steadfastness of Indian cultures themselves.

CHAPTER IX

FOOTNOTES

[1]Croix to Gálvez, No. 458, informe General, Arizpe, January 23, 1780, paragraph 3, AGI, Guadalajara 253; another copy in Guadalajara 522.

[2]Croix to Gálvez, No. 735, Informe General, Arizpe, April 23, 1782, paragraphs 4850, AGI Guadalajara 253; another copy in Guadalajara 279.

[3]Croix to Gálvez, No. 835, Informe sobre el estado de guerra, Arizpe, October 7, 1782, paragraph 82, AGI, Guadalajara 254.

[4]Ibid., paragraphs 118-37.

[5]Ibid., paragraphs 80-81.

[6]Elizondo to Viceroy Marqués de Croix, Pitic, November 5, 1769, AGI, Guadalajara 416.

[7]Governor Felipe de Barri, Resúmen general de las hostilidades . . . de esta provincia de la Nueva Vizcaya, 1771-1776, Durango, June 30, 1777 (enclosed with Barri to Gálvez, Durango, November 8, 1777) AGI, Guadalajara 274. See also Moorhead, The Presidio, 71-74, 178-83.

[8]Navarro García, Don José de Gálvez, 123-24. Regular units of Spanish infantry saw frontier service on an experimental basis. These regulars included a picket of fifty officers and men of the Infantería de América, a hundred dragoons of the Regimiento de España, another hundred dragoons of the Regimiento de Mexico, and a company of eighty Voluntarios de Cataluña. See María del Carmen Velásquez, El estado de guerra en Nueva España 1760-1808, 110-15.

[9]Bucareli, Estracto de Novedades, Mexico, November 26, 1774 (enclosed with Bucareli to Arriaga, No. 1614, same place and date), AGI, Guadalajara 514.

[10]Ibid.

[11]Bucareli, Estracto de Noticias, Mexico, March 27, 1776 (enclosed with Bucareli to Arriaga, No. 2178, same place and date), AGI, Guadalajara 515.

[12]Bucareli, Extracto de Novedades, Mexico, July 27, 1776 (enclosed with Bucareli to Gálvez, No. 2372, same place and date), and Bucareli, Extracto de Novedades, Mexico, September 26, 1776 (enclosed with Bucareli to Gálvez, No. 2495, same place and date), AGI, Guadalajara 515.

[13]Moorhead, The Presidio, 65, 70-71, 89.

[14]Commandant Inspector Hugo O'Conor, Extracto de la Revista de Inspección, San Buenaventura, January 27, 1774 (enclosed with Bucareli to Arriaga, No. 1312, Mexico, March 27, 1774), AGI, Guadalajara 513. For a detailed examination of another frontier garrison, Janos, see Paige W. Christiansen, "The Presidio and the Borderlands: A Case Study," Journal of the West 8 (January 1969): 29-37.

[15]Nicolás Gil, Hoja de servicios, June 28, 1778, AGI, Guadalajara 275.

[16]O'Conor, Extracto de la Revista de Inspección, San Buenaventura, January 27, 1774.

[17]Ibid.

[18]Ibid.

[19]Moorhead, The Presidio, 226-27.

[20]Ibid., 233-37; Reglamento de 1772, Title II, Articles 1-2.

[21]Croix to Captain Nicolás Gil, Instrucciones, Chihuahua, October 14, 1778, Articles 2-5 (enclosed with Croix to Gálvez, No. 297, Chihuahua, October 23, 1778), AGI, Guadalajara 270. In early 1779, Tarahumaras at San Buenaventura protested over the type of labor assigned and the small compensation received. Seeing no corrective measures taken, they abandoned the presidio and returned to their village. Croix to Gálvez, Informe General, July 29, 1781, paragraph 215, AGI, Guadalajara 279.

[22]Moorhead, The Presidio, 72.

[23]Ibid., 96; Brigadier Felipe de Neve to Gálvez, No. 89, Arizpe, March 8, 1778, (certified copy) AGI, Guadalajara 519.

[24]Neve to Gálvez, No. 101, Arizpe, April 5, 1784, AGI Guadalajara 519; Neve to Gálvez, No. 123, Fronteras, July 6, 1784, AGI, Guadalajara 520.

[25]Ibid.

[26]Son of Viceroy Matías de Gálvez and nephew of José de Gálvez, Bernardo de Gálvez served as New Spain's viceroy between 1785-86. Having campaigned in the north with his uncle's expeditionary force (1768-70), he was briefly a compañía volante captain, military commandant for both Nueva Vizcaya and Sonora, and military governor of Louisiana from 1777 to 1783. The viceroy fully comprehended that the perplexing situation in the Provincias Internas arose from the difficulty of dealing with a people friendly at times, hostile at others, but most often of uncertain disposition. Navarro García, Don José de Gálvez, 188-96, 452-55.

[27]Bernardo de Gálvez, Instrucción formado en virtud de Real Orden de S.M., que dirige al Señor Comandante General de Provincias Internas Don Jacobo Ugarte y Loyola para gobierno y puntual obervancia de este Superior Gefe de sus inmediatos subalternos, August 26, 1786, Articles 18-79, 153-54, 214, AGI, Guadalajara 268. For a translation accompanied by the orginal text, see Donald E. Worcester, ed., Instructions for Governing the Interior Provinces of New Spain, 1786, by Bernardo de Gálvez.

[28]Jacobo Ugarte to the Marqués de Sonora, Nos. 75, 77, 88, 104, Janos and Arizpe, March 20, April 16, May 14, and June 8, 1787, AGI, Guadalajara 287; Intendant Governor Pedro Corbalan, Informe General, Vera Cruz, March 8, 1788, AGN, PI 254, expediente 7.

[29]Ugarte to Viceroy Manuel Antonio Flores, Arizpe, October 1, 1787, AGN, PI 112, expediente 1.

[30]Croix to Gálvez, No. 458, Arizpe, January 23, 1780, paragraph 3, AGI, Guadalajara 253.

[31]Croix to Gálvez, No. 735, Informe General, Arizpe, April 23, 1782, paragraphs 48-49, AGI, Guadalajara 253.

[32]Croix to Gálvez, No. 835, Informe, Arizpe, October 7, 1782, paragraphs 80-81, AGI, Guadalajara 254, For a description of the soldado de cuera, see Max. L. Moorhead, "The Soldado de Cuera: Stalwart of the Spanish Borderlands," Journal of the West 8 (January 1969): 38-55.

[33]Croix to Gálvez, No. 8, Mexico, February 26, 1777, AGI, Guadalajara 516; Navarro García, Don José de Gálvez, 399.

CHAPTER X

CONCLUSION

A consistency of Spanish Indian policy characterized relations with the northern tribes. Despite their often-touted firearms and horses, Spanish militia, presidio, or Indian allies could not otherwise have survived and defeated the enemy. Constantly in need of frontier development, Hapsburg and Bourbon officials in the north very often based their actions on Spanish forms of political, economic, and social organization. Hence, mission expansion in northern New Spain attempted to modify Indian cultures as well as establish new religious beliefs.

Spanish success in northern New Spain involved Indian fighting Indian under presidial or mission influence, and more often than not, the Indian, not the Spaniard, defeated his own race. In northern New Spain, no real underlying unity existed among tribes, and Yaquis, Tarahumaras, Opatas, Seris, Pimas, and Pueblos took pleasure in helping the northerners defeat such traditionally hated foes as the Apaches who, in turn, aided presidials or missionaries in assimilating other tribesmen. Nothing resembling a broad, effective confederacy of Indian peoples joined by the common purpose of exterminating the foreign intruders threatened the crown in the north. Lipánes, Mescaleros, Tepehuanes, Tarahumaras, Pimas, and others fought each other at military request and under Spanish sponsorship, and Opatas and Pimas effectively incorporated into presidial companies battled against other tribes. Except for rebel resistance and several alliances stemming from military or geographical necessity, nothing indicated a significant Indian confederacy.

The Indian revolts and general resistance are not separate entities. Indeed, it seems doubtful that separation can be meaningfully applied in the northern provinces since resistance, assimilation, and revolts appeared complex in purpose. They asserted aspects of the old way of life more in defiance of frontier society than for any intrinsic worth, and during the early stage of contact with frontier society, Indian tribes sought to assimilate certain values from Spanish settlers and from the religious missions. The two traditions overlapped and continued in parallel development, and ensuing revolts, rather than expressions of separatism, were mainly military uprisings, with an overall spirit of reactionism. No mere responses to local conditions, Indian resistance in the northern provinces manifested a reaction to culture conflict on all levels, set in motion by the encompassing northerners. The establishment of missions, presidios, mines, and towns tore the northern tribes from their very roots and stripped them of traditional relationships. These encroaching frontier institutions, still struggling in their own right, forced Indian communities either to adapt or rebel, and as traditional tribal authority eroded or collapsed, younger contenders for power filled the void. Popé, Salvador Palma, Osebaca, Bernabé and Muni, managed a tenuous control over their following, but when a Luis of Sáric called for rebellion, their people, already fragmented and smoldering, willingly revolted.

The failure of the Indian revolts to stem northern expansion arises from several sometimes confusing circumstances. Indian leaders and their lieutenants, as indicated earlier, were "marginal men" caught between the tribal way of life and a developing Spanish society that offered many opportunities at the cost of accepting some frightening risks. For example, Luis of Sáric wanted both to destroy and preserve, to stage both demonstration and rebellion, to assert traditional dignity through martyrdom and, at the same time, eliminate Jesuit mission rule. The Indian's unclear assessment of this oncoming frontier society--traditionless, as it seemed to him--weakened his efforts, somewhat confused by reglamentos and royal orders, left him little room to negotiate a meaningful peace.

By the late eighteenth century, pacification of the northern tribes evolved into a coordinated twofold policy of peace by mission efforts and warfare against unyielding renegades, with adjustments made according to the particular type of resistance. Implementation of the many reglamentos strengthened both military effectiveness and Indian policy, and though the pacification program moved haltingly through a bureaucracy both slow and confusing, it Mexicanized many Indian tribes by 1821. Major uprisings like the Pima, Tepehuán, Yaqui, Tarahumara, Seri, Pueblo, or Yuma revolts no longer threatened to disrupt further northern colonizing in the northern provinces.

Missionized Indians relying on the regular orders for direction had little tactical power since dependence on mission patronage left them without sufficient resources of their own to struggle effectively against frontier society. Indians induced into the religious missions rebelled, but only when able to rely on some tribal leader powerful enough to challenge the mission fathers. The charismatic Popé represented such strength in the Pueblo Revolt, Luis of Sáric in the Pima rebellion, Salvador Palma in the Yuma uprising, Bernabé and Muni in the Yaqui Revolt and Ignacio Osebaca in the Tarahumara Revolt. With such personal stature present, tribesmen had latitude of movement; without it, they submitted to military or missionary constraints. Only when a tribal leader proved capable of dealing with the military or mission presence did they lend support to an uprising.

The spontaneous nature of Indian revolts leave no doubt that individual leaders inspired and led the rebellions. But frontier officials, quick to single out such instigators, learned by trial and error how to deal efficaciously with tribal leaders, relying on traditional tactics. Many tribes resisted the pressures of the alien presence, and there were many serious revolts against Spanish authority. Moreover, the expansion of their types of resistance, and finally, massive renegade activity in provinces like Sonora and Nueva Vizcaya created a problem for the Bourbon Crown. In the long run, the effort to exterminate renegade resistance worked to the advantage of the Spaniards, even given the many structural insufficiencies of the northern provinces. Spain could afford neither the bureaucracy nor the frontier army necessary for the task. But Indian cultures held to their way of life as long as they had enough numbers and capable leadership, and their tenacity in the face of unabating Spanish aggression lends stature to the history of the southwestern United States and the Mexican North.

ARCHIVAL SOURCES

Archivo General de Indias, Sevilla, Spain
    Audiencia de Guadalajara
            Legajos 7, 135-38, 143, 144, 145, 152, 164, 171, 188,
            194, 242, 153-55, 268, 270-72, 274-76, 278-79, 281, 283,
            285-87, 301, 416, 418-19, 511-20, 522, 578, 586.
    Audiencia de Mexico
            Legajos 270, 1369, and 2429.
    Indiferente General
            Legajos 102, 1526, 1713.

Archivo General de la Nación, Mexico City, Mexico
    Provincias Internas
            Tomos or Volúmenes (Legajos) 30, 36, 77, 87, 88, 112, 116, 170,
            254.
    Correspondencia de los Virreyes
            Tomo 25.
    Historia
            Tomo 24
    California
            Tomo 1 and 2
    Presidios
            Tomo 11

Spanish Archives of New Mexico, State of New Mexico Records Center, Sante Fe,
    New Mexico. Documents 110, 121, 340, 340a, 414, 438, 455, 495.

Archivo Hidalgo de Parral, Chihuahua, Mexico
    (Microcopy at the Special Collections Library, University of New Mexico,
    Albuquerque, New Mexico). Rolls 1692, 1697A, 1708b, 1710b, and
    1715Aa.

PUBLISHED DOCUMENTS

Alessio Robles, Vito., ed. Diario y derrotero de lo caminado, visto y observado en
    la visita que hizo a los presidios de la Nueva España Septentrional el
    Brigadier don Pedro de Rivera. Mexico, 1946.

Arricivita, Juan Domingo. Crónica Seráfica y Apostólica del Colegio de
    Propaganda Fide de la Santa Cruz de Querétaro de la Nueva España.
    Mexico, 1792.

Benavides, Alonso de. Fray Alonso de Benavides' Revised Memorial of 1634.
    Ed. by Frederick Webb Hodge, George P. Hammond, and Agapito Rey.
    Albuquerque, 1945.

Bolton, Herbert E., ed. Anza's California Expeditions. 5 vols. Berkeley, 1930.

-----. Athanse de Mézieres and the Louisiana-Texas Frontier, 1768-1780. 2 vols. Cleveland, 1914.

Colección de documentos para la historia de Hispano-América. 14 vols. Madrid, 1927-32.

Documentos para la Historia de Mexico. Series 4. 21 vols. Mexico, 1853-57.

Gálvez, Bernardo de. Instrucción formado en virtud de Real Orden de S.M., que dirige al Señor Comandante General de Provincas Internas Don Jacobo Ugarte y Loyola para gobierno y puntal observancia de este Superior Gefe de sus inmediatos subalternos. Mexico, 1786.

Gonzales Flores, Enrique and Almada, Francisco R., eds. Informe de Hugo O'Conor sobre el estado de las Provincas Internas del Norte, 1771-1776. Mexico, 1952.

Guadalajara, Tomas de. Historia de la tercera rebelión tarahumara. Ed. by Roberto Ramos. Chihuahua, 1950.

Hackett, Charles W., ed. Historical Documents Relating to New Mexico, Nueva Vizcaya, and Approaches Thereto, to 1773. 3 vols. Washington, 1923-37.

-----. The Revolt of the Pueblo Indians of New Mexico, Otermin's Attempted Reconquest, 1680-1682. 2 vols. Albuquerque, 1953.

Kinnaird, Lawrence, ed. The Frontiers of New Spain: Nicolas de Lafora's Description, 1766-1768. Berkeley, 1958.

Lafora, Nicolás de. Relación del viaje que hizo a los Presidios Internos situados en la frontera de la América Septentrional pertenciente al Rey de España. Ed. by Alessio Robles. Mexico, 1939.

Mota y Escobar, Alonso de la. Descripción geográfica de los reinos de Nueva Galicia, Nueva Vizcaya y Nuevo León. Ed. by Joaquín Ramírez Cabánas. Mexico, 1940.

Nentvig, S.J., Juan. Rudo Ensayo, A Description of Sonora and Arizona in 1764. Ed. by Alberto Francisco Pradeau and Robert R. Rasmussen. Tucson, 1980.

Recopilación de leyes de los reynos de las Indias. Edición facsimilar de la cuarta impresion hecha en Madrid el año 1791. 3 vols. Madrid, 1943.

Reglamento e instrucción para los presidios que se han de formar en la linea de frontera de la Nueva España, resuelto por el Rey Nuestro Señor en cédula de 10 de Septiembre de 1772. Madrid, 1772.

Reglamento para todos los presidios de las provincias internas de este Governación, ...Hecho por el Excmo. Señor Marqués de Casa-Fuerte, Vi-Rey, Governador, y Capitán General de estos Reynos. Mexico, 1729.

Tamarón y Romeral, Pedro. Demostración del vastísimo obispado de la Nueva Vizcaya, 1765. Durango, Sinaloa, Sonora, Arizona, Nuevo Mexico, Chihuahua y porciones de Texas, Coahuila y Zacatecas. Ed. by Vito Alessio Robles. Mexico, 1937.

Thomas, Alfredo B. Forgotten Frontiers: A Study of the Spanish Indian Policy of Don Juan Bautista de Anza Governor of New Mexico, 1777-1787. Norman, 1932.

----. The Plains Indians and New Mexico, 1751-1778: A Collection of Documents Illustrative of the History of the Eastern Frontier of New Mexico. Albuquerque, 1940.

----. Teodoro de Croix and the Northern Frontier of New Spain, 1776-1783. Norman, 1941.

Treutlein, Theodore E., ed. and trans. Ignaz Pfefferkorn: Sonora, A Description of the Province. Albuquerque, 1949.

----. Missionary in Sonora, The Travel Reports of Joseph Och, S.J. 1755-1767. San Francisco, 1965.

Velasco Ceballos, Rómulo, ed. La administración de D. Frey Antonio María de Bucareli y Ursua, cuadragesima sexto virrey de Mexico. 2 vols. Mexico, 1936.

Wilbur, Marquerite Eyler, ed. The Indian Uprising in Lower California, 1734-1737, as Described by Father Sigismundo Taravajal. Los Angeles, 1931.

Worcester, Donald E., ed. Instructions for Governing the Interior Provinces of New Spain, 1786, by Bernardo de Galvez. Berkeley, 1951.

UNPUBLISHED STUDIES

Ewing, Russell C. "The Pima Uprising, 1751-52: A Study in Spain's Indian Policy." Ph.D. dissertation, University of California, Berkeley, 1934.

Maughan, Scott Jarvis. "Francisco Garcés and New Spain's Northwestern Frontier, 1768-1781." Ph.D. dissertation, University of Utah, 1968.

Rowland, David Winslow. "The Elizondo Expedition Against the Indian Rebels of Sonora, 1765-1771." Ph.D. dissertation, University of California, Berkeley, 1930.

ARTICLES

Adams, Eleanor B., ed. "Bishop Tamarón's Visitation of New Mexico, 1760,"
part 2, New Mexico Historical Review 28 (July 1953): 192-221.

Bolton, Herbert E. "The Mission as a Frontier Institution in the Spanish-American
Colonies," American Historical Review 23 (October 1917): 42-61.

Chávez, Angelico. "Pohe-Yemo's Representative and the Pueblo Revolt of 1680,"
New Mexico Historical Review 42 (April 1967): 85-126.

Christiansen, Paige W. "The Presidio and the Borderlands: A Case Study,"
Journal of the West 8 (January 1969): 29-37.

Ewing, Russell C. "Investigations into the Causes of the Pima Uprising of 1751,"
Mid-America 23 (April 1941): 138-51.

----. "The Pima Outbreak in November, 1751," New Mexico Historical Review 8
(1938): 337-46.

----. "The Pima Uprising of 1751," in Greater America: Essays in Honor of
Herbert E. Bolton. Los Angeles, 1945, pp. 259-80.

Hernández y Sánchez-Barba, Mario. "Frontera, Población y Milicia (Estudio
estructural de la acción defensiva hispanica en Sonora durante el siglo
XVIII)," Revista de Indias 63 (1956): 9-49.

Kessell, John L. "The Making of a Martyr: The Young Francisco Garcés," New
Mexico Historical Review 45 (July 1970): 181-96.

Moore, Mary Lu and Beene, Delmar L., eds. "The Interior Provinces of New
Spain: The Report of Hugo O'Conor, January 30, 1776," Arizona and
West 13 (1971): 265-82.

Moorhead, Max L. "The Soldado de Cuera: Stalwart of the Spanish Borderlands,"
Journal of the West 8 (January 1969): 38-55.

Mosk, Sanford A. "Economic Problems in Sonora in the Late Eighteenth Century,"
Pacific Historical Review 8 (September 1939) 341-46.

Park, John F. "Spanish Indian Policy in Northern Mexico, 1765-1810," Arizona
and the West 4 (Winter 1962): 325-44.

Poole, Stafford R. "War by Fire and Blood," The Americas 22 (October 1965):
115-37.

Reeve, Frank. "Navajo-Spanish Diplomacy, 1770-1790," New Mexico Historical
Review 35 (July 1960): 200-35.

Sánchez, Jane C. "Spanish-Indian Relations During the Otermín Administration," New Mexico Historical Review 58 (April 1983): 133-51.

Sanchiz Ochoa, Pilar. "La Población indígena del noroeste de Mexico in el siglo XVIII: algunos cuestiones en torno a la demografía y aculturación," Revista Española de Antropología Americana 7 (1972): 95-126.

Schmutz, Richard. "Jesuit Missionary Methods in Northwestern Mexico," Journal of the West 8 (January 1969): 76-89.

Scholes, France V. "Civil Government and Society in New Mexico in the Seventeenth Century," New Mexico Historical Review 10 (January 1935): 71-111.

Thomas, Alfred B. "A Description of Sonora in 1772," Arizona Historical Review 5 (1932-33): 302-307.

Treutlein, Theodore E. "The Economic Regime of the Jesuits in Eighteenth-Century Sonora," Pacific Historical Review 8 (September 1939): 289-300.

Vigness, David M. "Don Hugo O'Conor and New Spain's Northeastern Frontier, 1764-1776," Journal of the West 6 (January 1967): 28-35.

Worcester, Donald E. "The Spread of Spanish Horses in the Southwest," New Mexico Historical Review 20 (January 1945): 1-13.

BOOKS

Alegre, Francisco, Javier. S.J. Historia de la Compañía de Jesús en Nueva España. 3 vols. México, 1842.

Alessio Robles, Vito. Coahuila y Texas en la epoca colonial. 2 vols. Mexico, 1938.

Almada, Francisco R. Diccionario de historia, geografía y biografía sonorenses. Chihuahua, 1952.

Archer, Christon I. The Army in Bourbon Mexico, 1760-1810. Albuquerque, 1977.

Bakewell, P.J. Silver Mining and Society in Mexico: Zacatecas 1546-1700. Cambridge, 1971.

Bannon, John Francis. Bolton and the Spanish Borderlands. Norman, 1964.

Beals, Ralph L. The Comparative Ethnology of Northern Mexico Before 1750. Ibero-Americana: No. 2. Berkeley, 1932.

Beilharz, Edwin A. Felipe de Neve, First Governor of California. San Francisco, 1971.

Bobb, Bernard E. The Viceregency of Antonio María Bucareli in New Spain, 1771-1779. Austin, 1962.

Bolton, Herbert E. Texas in the Middle Eighteenth Century: Studies in Spanish Colonial History and Administration. New York, 1962.

Brinckerhoff, Sidney B. and Faulk, Odie B. Lancers for the King: A Study of the Frontier Military System of Northern New Spain, with a Translation of the Royal Regulations of 1772. Phoenix, 1965.

Castañeda, Carlos E. Our Catholic Heritage in Texas, 1519-1936. 7 vols. Austin, 1936-50.

Chapman, Charles E. A History of California: The Spanish Period. New York, 1923.

Chevalier, Francois. Land and Society in Colonial Mexico. Ed. by Lesley Byrd Simpson. Berkeley, 1966.

Dobyns, Henry F. Spanish Colonial Tucson. Tucson, 1976.

Dunne, Peter Masten. Black Robes in Lower California. Berkeley, 1952.

----. Early Jesuit Missions in Tarahumara. Berkeley, 1948.

Forbes, Jack D. Apache, Navaho, and Spaniard. Norman, 1960.

----. Warriors of the Colorado: The Yumas of the Quechan Nation and Their Neighbors. Norman, 1965.

Galaviz de Capdevielle, María Elena. Rebeliones indígenes en el norte de la Nueva España, siglos XVI y XVII. Mexico, 1967.

Gallegos, José Ignacio. Durango Colonial, 1563-1821. Mexico, 1967.

Hanke, Lewis. The Spanish Struggle for Justice in the Conquest of America. Philadelphia, 1949.

Hernández y Sánchez-Barba, Mario. La última expansión española en América. Madrid, 1957.

Hodge, Frederick W., ed. Handbook of the American Indians North of Mexico. 2 vols. Washington, 1907-10.

Huerta Preciado, María Teresa. Rebeliones índigenas en el Noreste de Mexico en la época colonial. Mexico, 1963.

Hu-De Hart, Evelyn. Missionaries, Miners, and Indians. Tucson, 1981.

John, Elizabeth A. H. Storms Brewed in Other Men's Worlds: The Confrontation of Indians, Spanish and French in the Southwest, 1540-1795. College Station, 1975.

Jones, Oakah L., Jr. Pueblo Warriors and Spanish Conquest. Norman, 1966.

Kessell, John L. Friars, Soldiers, and Reformers, Hispanic Arizona and the Sonora Mission Frontier, 1767-1856. Tucson, 1976.

----. Mission of Sorrows: Jesuit Guevavi and the Pimas, 1691-1767. Tucson, 1970.

Moorhead, Max L. The Apache Frontier: Jacobo Ugarte and Spanish-Indian Relations in Northern New Spain, 1769-1791. Norman, 1968.

----. The Presidio: Bastion of the Spanish Borderlands. Norman, 1975.

Navarro García, Luis. Don José de Gálvez y la Comandancia General de las Provincias Internas del Norte de Nueva España. Sevilla, 1964.

----. La Sublevación Yaqui de 1740. Sevilla, 1966.

Polzer, Charles W. Rules and Precepts of the Jesuit Missions of Northwestern New Spain. Tucson, 1976.

Porras Múñoz, Gillermo. La Frontera con los Indios de Nueva Vizcaya en el Siglo XVII. Mexico, 1980.

Powell, Philip W. Mexico's Miguel Caldera, The Taming of America's First Frontier, 1548-1579. Tucson, 1977.

----. Soldiers, Indians, and Silver: The Northward Advance of New Spain, 1550-1600. Berkeley and Los Angeles, 1962.

Ricard, Robert. The Spiritual Conquest of Mexico: An Essay on the Evangelizing Methods of the Mendicant Orders in New Spain: 1532-1572. Trans. by Lesley Byrd Simpson. Berkeley and Los Angeles, 1966.

Richardson, Rupert N. The Comanche Barrier to the South Plains Settlement. Glendale, 1934.

Sauer, Carl. The Distribution of Aboriginal Tribes and Languages in Northwestern Mexico. Ibero-Americana: No. 5. Berkeley, 1934.

Scholes, France V. Troublous Times in New Mexico, 1659-1670. Albuquerque, 1942.

Spicer, Edward H. Cycles of Conquest: The Impact of Spain, Mexico, and the
    United States on the Indians of the Southwest, 1533-1960. Tucson, 1962.

Twitchell, Ralph E. The Spanish Archives of New Mexico. 2 vols. Cedar Rapids,
    1914.

Velásquez, María del Carmen. El estado de guerra en Nueva España, 1760-1808.
    Mexico, 1950.

Weddle, Robert S. San Juan Bautista: Gateway to Spanish Texas. Austin, 1968.

INDEX

Acaxee Revolt, 21-22
Anza, Gov. Juan Bautista de, 2, 5, 86, 100, 100-103, 106
Arce y Arroyo, Gov. Pablo, 77
Barri, Gov. Felipe, 100
Becerro, Seri Leader, 75
Benavides, Father Alonso de, 36
Berroterán, Capt. José de, 72
Bolson de Mapimí, 11, 38, 45, 70, 72, 91, 100
Boquinete, Seri Leader, 100-101, 114
Bourbon Indian Policy, 43-44, 69, 85, 88, 99-101, 103, 107
Bucareli, Viceroy Antonio María, 88-91, 93, 101-104, 107
Bustamente, Gov. Juan Domingo de, 71
Cabello Largo, Lipán chieftan, 92
Caddos, 43, 52, 90
Castillo, Gov. Gabriel del, 26, 39-41, 45
Catiti, Alonso, 37
Chichimecas, 19-21, 42, 126
Chigoynare, Indian Gov. of Nahuerachic, 40
Chiricahuas, 6, 114
Coahuila, province of, 12
Cogoxito, Tepehuán Leader, 21-22, 74
Compañías volantes, 12, 89, 123, 128
Council of the Indies, 28
Croix, Caballero Teodoro de, 2, 20, 99-107, 113, 121-124, 126-128
Detribalized Indians, 13, 79
Díaz, Capt. Domingo, 2, 91, 100
Díaz, Father Juan, 105, 103-105
Elizondo, Col. Domingo, 86, 122
Fages, Col. Pedro, 106
Fajardo, Gov. Diego Guajardo, 23
Fayni, Gov. José de, 88, 90
Figueroa, Father Geronimo, 59, 60

Fonte, Father Juan, 22
Franciscan mission program, 35-36, 52-54
French-Indian trade, 44, 72
Gálvez, Viceroy Bernardo de, 2, 117, 127
Gálvez, José de, 2, 75, 85-86, Minister of the Indies, 88-89, 93, 99
Garcés, Father Francisco, 2, 102-105, 107
Gil, Capt. Nicolás, 2, 123, 124, 125
Gileños, 5, 45, 70, 88, 91; alliances, 100, 102-103; organized resistance, 113-114, 127
Guadalajara, Father Tomás, 62
Guerra de fuego y a sangre, 4, 20-21
Hacendados, definition of, 2
Hapsburg Indian Policy, 19-21, 35, 58
Hechiceros. See Shamans
Hernandez, Antonio (Alias El Mordullo), 114
Hostinsky, Father George, 40-41
Huidobro, Capt. Manuel Bernal de, 73-74
Hurdaide, Diego de, 21
Ibarguen, Raphael de, 24
Ignacio, Yuma Leader, 104-105, 107
Illink, Father Wilhelm, 40
Indian bands: Chinipas, 21; Chisos, 70; Conchos, 5, 38-41; Faraón, 45; Jovas, 42, 55; Jumanos, 52; Mogolloñes, 6, 114; Salineros, 5, 21; Tamaulipas, 5; Tobosos, 5, 21, 38, 41, 56; Tontos, 6; Tortugas, 5; Venados, 5; Xiximes, 21
Indios amigos, 19-20, 41, 62, 73, 78, 88-89, 123, 127
Instrucción de 1786, 117
Islas, Ensign Santiago de, 104, 105, 107
Jabanimó, Pima Leader, 78